But Can I Start a Sentence with "But"?

Chicago Guides
to *Writing*, Editing,
and Publishing

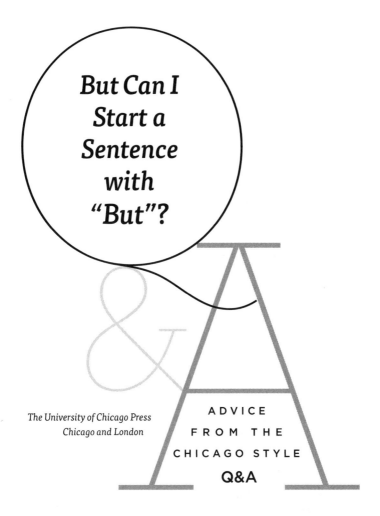

But Can I Start a Sentence with "But"?

& A

ADVICE FROM THE CHICAGO STYLE Q&A

The University of Chicago Press
Chicago and London

The University of Chicago Press Editorial Staff

WITH A FOREWORD BY CAROL FISHER SALLER

The University of Chicago Press, Chicago 60637
The University of Chicago Press, Ltd., London
© 2016 by The University of Chicago
All rights reserved. Published 2016.
Printed in the United States of America

25 24 23 22 21 20 19 18 17 16   1 2 3 4 5

ISBN-13: 978-0-226-37064-4 (cloth)
ISBN-13: 978-0-226-37078-1 (e-book)
DOI: 10.7208/chicago/9780226370781.001.0001

Library of Congress Cataloging-in-Publication Data

Names: University of Chicago. Press.
Title: But can i start a sentence with "but"? : advice from the Chicago
    style Q&A / the University of Chicago Press editorial staff ; with a
    foreword by Carol Fisher Saller.
Other titles: Chicago guides to writing, editing, and publishing.
Description: Chicago ; London : The University of Chicago Press,
    2016. | Series: Chicago guides to writing, editing, and publishing
Identifiers: LCCN 2015037942 | ISBN 9780226370644 (cloth : alk.
    paper) | ISBN 9780226370781 (e-book)
Subjects: LCSH: Authorship—Handbooks, manuals,
    etc. | Authorship—Style manuals.
Classification: LCC PN147 .B88 2016 | DDC 808.02/7—dc23 LC record
    available at http://lccn.loc.gov/2015037942

♾ This paper meets the requirements of ANSI/NISO Z39.48-1992
(Permanence of Paper).

Editing might be a bloody trade.
But knives aren't the exclusive property of
butchers. Surgeons use them too.

BLAKE MORRISON

Contents

Foreword

Since 1997, readers of *The Chicago Manual of Style*'s website have been submitting style and grammar questions to the Q&A page that is updated each month by manuscript editors at the University of Chicago Press. Before there was a website, we occasionally answered questions over the phone. Not that we actively solicited such queries; in fact, to be honest, they could be a little annoying. After all, it takes a certain amount of chutzpah to call up a major university press and expect an editor there to stop what she's doing and determine whether *nonfat* takes a hyphen. (It doesn't.) Nevertheless, that's what we used to do, at no charge. A bonus for us was that sometimes we ended up having interesting conversations with curious strangers who cared as much as we did about a point of grammar or about formatting a citation properly. Occasionally, a conversation led to an improvement in the recommendations we offer in the *Manual*.

After we discontinued the phone-query service and invited the entire planet to seek our advice online, demand quickly exceeded our ability to answer and still meet our deadlines. So we decided to choose a few of the most interesting questions and answer them in a monthly online Q&A. The posted questions and answers go into an archive that is searchable to anyone with an Internet connection. The archive contains only questions that were featured in the Q&A; regrettably, many more remain unanswered. We are often asked why we don't provide a help line to serve a greater number of readers. The answer is simple: all our advice is given by senior editors with years of experience at the Press—"power users" of *CMOS* who have personally assisted with revising the *Manual* into new editions. They already have their hands full editing the more than three hundred new books we publish each year, and we aren't willing to settle for helpers with less expertise.

As you might imagine, among the questions readers submit, we get some doozies. *The Chicago Manual of Style*'s thousand-plus pages of style and grammar and citation guidelines can bewilder a person whose teacher or boss drops the book on their desk and says, "Follow this." We do our best to help: The book (both print and online) has detailed tables of contents at the start of each chapter. It has a killer index. The online edition is fully searchable, and there's a free online "Quick Guide" that gives examples of how to cite many of the most common types of sources as a note or in a bibliography. And yet we get questions. Endless, inventive, heartbreaking. Reading through the questions in this book, you will see for yourself the range of topics addressed, the diverse experience of the questioners, and the ease or difficulty with which we articulate our answers.

This book is arranged in categories that loosely reflect those on the Browse Q&A page at *CMOS Online*. The categories at the website have accumulated willy-nilly over the years and admittedly range from helpful to tongue-in-cheek. Since many of the questions fall into more than one category, the best way to find all the Q&As in this book that touch on a specific subject is to consult the index at the back of the book.

Finally, a caveat: over the years, the Q&A has developed

a . . . voice. It's not that we set out to be cheeky. We have boundless and sincere empathy for anyone who struggles with using what readers affectionately call the "Big Orange" (for its signature tomato-red cover), and we can't help but respect those who are motivated to find our site and send us a question. But occasionally—mostly in the rush of trying to answer as many questions as we can in spare time that is truly spare—we snap.

Fortunately for us, our readers are loyal, forgiving, and fun-loving. Tens of thousands subscribe to the monthly e-mail alert that a new Q&A list has been posted, and many write to express delight and appreciation. And even though the content presented in this book is available online, we regularly receive requests for a *Best of the Q&A* book.

Here it is—thank you for asking! (And yes, you can start a sentence with *but*.)

Carol Fisher Saller, Q&A Editor
CHICAGO MANUAL OF STYLE ONLINE

CHAPTER ONE

"It's not so much an issue of correctness as of ickiness"

....

ABBREVIATIONS, ACRONYMS, AND INITIALISMS ✶
COMPOUNDS ✶ NUMBERS ✶ PLURALS ✶ POSSESSIVES AND
ATTRIBUTIVES ✶ WORDS AND LETTERS

....

So much of editing goes beyond merely applying rules. It requires judgment. "Correctness" is taken for granted as a goal—but correctness according to whom? What's correct in a legal document might be a big mistake in a graphic novel or blog post. For good reason, writers live in fear of overzealous copyeditors who, in search of correctness, will edit the life and voice right out of their work.

Correctness can be especially elusive when dictionaries, style guides, and usage manuals disagree. There is more general agreement on matters of *grammar* than on matters of *style*, such as punctuation, hyphenation, capitalization, or abbreviation. In style matters, there are often competing options, all acceptable. And when personal preferences come into play—when my "correct" is your "ick"—style choices can get tricky.

Abbreviations, Acronyms, and Initialisms

Q. My significant other and I have a disagreement: he maintains that in referring to a roomful of nurses, we may say "a roomful of R.N." on the grounds that we do not need to pluralize R.N. as R.N.s, although he does concede that one would not say "a roomful of nurse." ("Room full" perhaps irrationally connotes to me a more ominous density of nurses than "roomful.") We have been arguing about this for going-on ten years and would like to settle the question in order to move on to some new dispute.

A. To my ear, a roomful of RN sounds far more ominous than a roomful of RNs. But as you can see, Chicago style regularly pluralizes abbreviations and skips the pesky periods: "a roomful [or room full] of RNs." Maybe you can argue about the periods from now on.

....

Q. I am editing a manuscript of a law book that uses many specialized abbreviations. There is a table of abbreviations, but we have decided to spell out each abbreviation the first time it is used in each chapter, followed by the abbreviation in parentheses. The only question I have is regarding abbreviations for commonly known words. For example, the author lists the United States in the table of abbreviations. To be consistent, I have spelled out United States the first time it is used and followed it with (US). This strikes me as kind of silly, as everyone knows that the US is the United States. Any suggestions?

A. Yes, I agree that explaining abbreviations like US is unnecessary. When consistency gets silly, you can rebel.

Q. I am editing a dissertation for a client who wants to use an abbreviation *N.* in place of *Nietzsche* in a dissertation on Nietzsche. Her advisor said this is okay. I told her it is not okay, and that abbreviations, explained in a list of abbreviations, should be used only for titles of works or for author's names if they are used in citations but not in the text itself. Am I right?

A. If the author's dissertation advisor approves, I don't see why we should object. After all, it's possible that no one besides those two will even read this opus. But if the motive is merely to save typing that wretched name a million times, it would be easy enough to type *N.* and then replace all the initials with a careful search-and-replace action. If the work is ever revised for publication, the name should be spelled out.

....

Q. I am proofing an engineering document. There is a section titled "System Engineering Instruction Team (SEIT)." However, this acronym is already defined in the body of a previous section. The argument is that the section in question should simply be titled "SEIT." However, I don't think the section title should be reduced to "SEIT" because the reader may not know what SEIT means upon first glance at the table of contents. I say it's okay to redefine the acronym if it suddenly becomes the title of a major section. Is it ever okay to redefine an acronym after it has already been defined?

A. Of course it's okay! What good is a rule that says you can't help the reader when it seems like a good idea? Redefine an acronym whenever a reader might reasonably have forgotten it.

Q. Dear *CMOS*, I've often encountered "business process outsourcing" abbreviated to BPO whether it's used as a noun or as an adjective. To my ear, the abbreviation is fine as an adjective but sounds awkward when used and read as a noun, in which case I use the full form. For example, "The company provides IT support and BPO services"—fine. "The company provides services in IT support and business process outsourcing"—fine. "The company provides services in IT support and BPO"—awkward. Is it just me, or does this preference have a sound grammatical basis?

A. It's just you. *Outsourcing* is a noun, so there's nothing wrong with using the initialism as a noun. If your readers are used to the abbreviation, then by spelling it out you are probably just slowing them down.

....

Q. When we first use an acronym or initialism like FMCSA we put it in parentheses after the spelled-out version. If the spelled-out version is possessive, does the acronym/initialism need to be possessive too? Example: the Federal Motor Carrier Safety Administration's (FMCSA's) new rule *or* the Federal Motor Carrier Safety Administration's (FMCSA) new rule?

A. This question is surely one of the most frequently asked; in the next edition of *The Chicago Manual of Style* I hope we will issue an explicit ban on this construction. In the meantime, please avoid using a possessive in the word before a parenthesis: the new rule issued by the Federal Motor Carrier Safety Administration (FMCSA).

Q. When you have an initialism, do you cap the first letter of each word when the phrase is completely spelled out?

A. In the spelled-out version, simply cap as you would if an initialism did not exist: standard operating procedures (SOPs), Rhode Island (RI), *American Journal of Education* (*AJE*), Mothers against Preschoolers (MAP).

....

Q. When you write about a GIF in a text, can you just refer to it as a GIF on first reference or do you have to write "graphic interchange format (GIF)"? I don't think the long version is actually helpful; more people know it as GIF. And I'd be using it as a noun.

A. You never have to do anything that isn't helpful. If a style guide says you do, you need a better guide.

Compounds

Q. When I entered an incorrect password for your website, I received this message: "Invalid Log In." Shouldn't "log in" be "login" in this case?

A. In a world where *CMOS* editors could stand with whips and chains over all the IT teams who write code for error messages for all the software packagers who supply all the websites, everything would be written consistently in Chicago style. As it is, however, *CMOS* editors have no such power. And quite honestly? We're fine with that.

Q. Can you resolve an apparent contradiction concerning compounds? The term in question is *copyeditor*. According to section 7.85, *copyeditor* seems to be classified as a "permanent compound." Section 7.78 offers the following definition of that term: "A permanent compound is one that has been accepted into the general vocabulary and can be found in the dictionary." Yet www.merriam-webster.com (a recommended resource in the *CMOS* bibliography) has *copy editor*. I've seen the Q&A answer that guesses at the justification of the noun *copyeditor* on the basis of *copyediting* as a verb. And I do agree with you that there are more worthy issues to tackle. Just wondering if there is something we're missing in the apparent contradiction.

A. To clarify, Chicago style is not the same as *Merriam-Webster's*; rather, we recommend that dictionary when a particular word or construction is not covered in *CMOS*. *Copyeditor* has been Chicago's preference since the 14th edition. Naturally, dictionaries and style manuals sometimes disagree—after all, who gets to decide what has been "accepted into the general vocabulary"?

....

Q. I am a primary teacher. I am currently teaching about compound words and have discovered that I am making errors. Some words that I thought were compound are not. However, when I look them up in different sources or look at signs, they are written both as compounds and closed. Would you please tell me how I can find a list of compound words without looking up each word in the dictionary? Thank you.

A. Although an online searchable dictionary would be a good tool for this purpose, the study of compounds is an awfully advanced topic for primary schoolchildren. Adult writers and copyeditors struggle with this issue; I doubt that seven-year-olds can handle it. Most compounds have more than one correct styling. As you've discovered, one dictionary will close up words, and another won't. Even more confusing is that some compounds are hyphenated only when they serve as a modifying phrase. If you must discuss compounds and hyphenation, it would be better to teach your children how to use a dictionary. Show them that dictionaries disagree. Encourage them to use their own judgment in choosing and then to be consistent. Older children can be taught to read a sentence for sense to see whether a compound benefits from a hyphen.

....

Q. There's a club for people who've worked at my office for twenty-five or more years. It is called the Twenty-Five Year Club. I am wondering why they never added a hyphen between *five* and *year* and also if it's okay to retain the capital letters for all the words that are hyphenated. I don't want to rock the boat around here for a club that's been in existence longer than all of us have been in the Publications Office. We are preparing the program for their annual dinner and latest round of inductees. Should we let them retain their old name? Has this come up in other places?

A. Yes, it often comes up in the titles of works. Chicago style would be Twenty-Five-Year Club. As for rocking the boat, maybe Dear Abby has a website you can write to.

Numbers

Q. When should the written version of a number not be followed by that number in parentheses?

A. Hmm. In a love note? "Remitted herein please find three (3) little words . . ."

....

Q. I am taking a college course in copyediting. My professor and I were having a discussion and I would like to know who is correct. We were presented with this sentence for correction: Of the 400 members, about 300 were over 60 years old, but at least 50 were under the age of 30. I understand the rules stated in 9.2 and 9.4 would apply here and require all of the numbers to be spelled out. However, I chose to leave the 60 and 30 in numerical form in accordance with 9.7, "To avoid a thickly clustered group of spelled-out numbers, numerals may be used instead in exception to the general rule." There are no guidelines that state when to apply the exception, nor are there examples to lead me to a definitive answer. Help please. How do you decide?

A. Your editing would make it easier for some readers to take in the numbers, while others would be distracted by a perceived inconsistency. That is a fundamental challenge for editors. You decide based on how consistent the text is to begin with, how much work it will be to carry out a change throughout a document, and how likely it is that you'll end up introducing inconsistencies. You weigh the work and the dangers against what you think most readers will find helpful. There's usually no "correct" winner; it's a judgment call.

Q. A colleague writes: "Basement space is about 5,700 square feet, but about 12,000 square feet is available on the eighth floor." I suspect the point is arguable, but couldn't that be "12,000 square feet *are* available on the eighth floor"?

A. Although it might seem counterintuitive, quantities of weight or measure are considered singular: five dollars is enough; three cups of flour makes one loaf. When you think about it, "12,000 square feet are available" reads as though someone short of cash could buy just one or two of them.

....

Q. Hi, *CMOS* people—I can't quite seem to figure out whether I should use spelled-out numbers or numerals with units of time—for example, seconds, minutes, hours, days, months, years. I am not sure whether it should be "2 to 4 weeks" or "two to four weeks"; "30 years" or "thirty years"; etc. I think for numbers over 99, numerals are used, for example "230 seconds." I understand that numerals should be used with units of measure in general, like kg, cm, °C, and °F, etc. Thank you for your help.

A. For units of time (or any other measure) in nontechnical text, we like to spell out numbers up to and including one hundred: "The cake burned in forty-one minutes." If, however, in a given paragraph the same time unit involves a mixture of numbers under and over one hundred, we style them all the same: "Ten runners clocked in at 94 minutes, and forty-three more finished in 101 minutes." (Note that the numbers of runners are not changed to numerals because in that category there is no inconsistency in styling them according to the rule.)

Numerals are always used with abbreviated measures like the ones you list, and in technical or statistical texts, numerals are used even when measures are spelled out. Sometimes even nontechnical text will have a passage containing many numerical references, in which case the editor might decide to use numerals for all in order to save space and prevent what might seem to be inconsistencies. See *CMOS* 16, chapter 9, for a detailed discussion.

. . . .

Q. Is it correct to say $3–5 million? Or should it be $3 to $5 million? Or $3 million to $5 million?

A. These are all acceptable ways to express the same thing. With regard to the $ symbol with inclusive numbers, in Chicago style an abbreviation or symbol is repeated if it is closed up to a number but not if it is separated by a space: $3–$5 million, but 2 × 5 in.

. . . .

Q. Do you have a policy about this pet peeve of mine? I think it is fine to write something like "My office hours are 10–11 AM," but it really seems wrong when the en dash is used in place of the word *and* or *to*. How can we make the world stop writing "My office hours are from 10–11 AM" or "My office hours are between 10–11 AM"?

A. We do have such a policy! (Please see *CMOS* 6.78.) Unfortunately, we have no way to make the world follow it.

Plurals

Q. My question refers to the plural use of acronyms and initialisms. As I have always understood it, the acronym or initialism can be pluralized only if the last letter indicates the plural item. So MOU (memorandum/memoranda of understanding) cannot become MOUs, but ICT can become ICTs (information and communication technologies). I run into this problem a lot with the initialism RFP (request for proposals), which people like to pluralize as RFPs to indicate multiple requests. The word *proposals* is already plural, so it does not make sense to me to add an *s* to the end of the initialism. What is the correct way to make acronyms or initialisms plural?

A. If you can stop thinking of the spelled-out meaning of the acronym and just treat the acronym itself as a word with its own meaning, you should be able to add that little *s* without fretting.

....

Q. The editors at our institution disagree about whether the singular *point* or plural *points* should be used in the following phrase: "0.4 percentage point(s)." Can you be the decider, as our commander-in-chief would say, on this one?

A. *Chicago Tribune* language writer Nathan Bierma made sense of this conundrum in a reply to a similar question. He quoted Bill Walsh of the *Washington Post*, who suggests that the trouble resides in thinking of the singular as one or less, whereas it's more helpful to think of the singular as exactly one, neither more nor less. Walsh points out that we say "zero dollars," not "zero dollar." By this logic, you should write "0.4 percentage points."

Q. I am editing a textbook for English students in Brazil. One of the exercises presents a recipe for pumpkin pie. Students are told the pie filling contains 1½ cup pumpkin, 1½ cup sugar, and so on. I seem to remember that anything greater than 1 should be plural. Am I correct? In other words, should the recipe read 1½ cups?

A. Yes, make those measures plural—but that's way too much sugar.

....

Q. Is it correct to use parenthesis to indicate the possibility of a noun as singular or plural? Example: Child(ren).

A. I wouldn't do it. It's not so much an issue of correctness as of ickiness.

....

Q. The February 2012 issue of *National Geographic* has a headline and subtitle that read, "What Dogs Tell Us: The ABC's of DNA." While I realize that *National Geographic* may have their own style guide, would Chicago style eliminate that apostrophe from *ABC's*?

A. We would. But that apostrophe is conventional in newspaper and magazine publishing. You'll probably see it everywhere, now that you've noticed it. In newspapers and magazines, where headlines often appear in all caps, the plurals of acronyms and initialisms without apostrophes (PCS, IVS, RBIS) would be difficult to interpret, since the final *S* would appear to be part of the acronym.

Q. In a policy, I have to indicate that the word *facility* could be plural. The person editing the document has written it as *facility(s)*. What is the correct way to portray nouns that end in *y* when necessary to indicate they could be singular or plural?

A. "Facility or facilities" and "one or more facilities" are both clear. And often the simple singular does just fine in implying one or more: "In the event that your facility is struck by terrorists, this contract is void." You can see that if two facilities were struck by terrorists, the clause would apply to both.

....

Q. Hello, Wise Ones. If you were me, how would you pluralize B-26? B-26es? B-26s? (Not, I'm pretty sure, B-26's.) None of them look right to me.

A. If we were you, of course, none of them would look right. But since we are *CMOS*, *B-26s* looks just fine. Please see *CMOS* 9.54.

Possessives and Attributives

Q. I am agitated about the institutional inconsistency on this point and found the College Board to be of no help, so I turn to you. What is the proper treatment of an associate degree? As I have stated it, or is it "associates" or "associate's"?

A. Someday someone will do something about institutional inconsistency, and then we can all retire. Meanwhile, both "associate degree" and "associate's degree" are widely used, and they both seem reasonable and logical. Even if the board never decides on one or the other, you can.

. . . .

Q. When referring to the house belonging to my wife and me, I have trouble deciding between "Libby and my house" or "Libby's and my house." Which is correct?

A. "Libby's and my house." In some contexts, the difference could be critical. You might not want to say, for instance, "We put Libby and my house on the market."

. . . .

Q. When forming the possessive for a proper noun rendered with an initialism, should I use 's, or, because the last word rendered by the initialism is "Services," should I treat it as a noun plural in form but singular in meaning, and add the apostrophe only? My instinct is to write "FIS's customers" because, plural services or no, FIS is one company. However, on that company's website I see that they form the possessive with the apostrophe only: "FIS' competitive edge." Thank you for any advice.

A. Your instincts are right: when you are working with initialisms, the trick is to ignore what the letters stand for. In your case, you are no longer talking about Friendly and Ineffectual Services' customers; you're talking about FIS's customers.

. . . .

Q. In section 6.23 of the 16th edition, the following example is used to illustrate an appositive with a comma: "Ursula's son, Clifford, had been a student of Norman Maclean's." I know that the usage displayed in the last three words of the sentence has become mainstream, but surely it has not become correct?

A. The double genitive (or double possessive) has long been correct. Even the old *Fowler's Modern English Usage* included it among the "sturdy indefensibles": that is, constructions that may be illogical and ungrammatical, but are idiomatic nonetheless. Fowler quotes its use in the opening lines of Shakespeare's *Antony and Cleopatra*: "Nay but this dotage of our general's o'erflows the measure." (You can find this in *Fowler's* under *of*, section 7: "Some freaks of idiom.") Burchfield's *Fowler's* (s.v. "double possessive") points out that the construction can serve a useful purpose, allowing us to distinguish between, say, "a picture of the king's" and "a picture of the king."

....

Q. I'm trying to find a definitive answer to whether an inanimate object can take the possessive form. I have been told that an object cannot possess something, so the 's form should not be used. Instead of "the vehicle's speed," it should be "the speed of the vehicle." I understand the rule, but can't find anything here to support it.

A. Let's think about it. If a table can't "have" legs, where does this leave us? True, the table is probably not conscious that it possesses legs, but then does that mean it doesn't truly possess them? If a table possesses legs in the forest, where there's no one to see them . . . oh, wait—that's another riddle. Seriously, I'd love to know who makes up these rules, seemingly just to drive everyone crazy. Don't worry—your vehicle can have speed, and there's no difference between the speed of the vehicle and the vehicle's speed (or "vehicle speed," if you prefer to avoid the controversy).

....

Q. If a phrase is possessive in the first instance it is used, is the abbreviation possessive as well? For example, should it be "Student Psychological Help Line's (SPHL) 24/7 assistance center" or "Student Psychological Help Line's (SPHL's) 24/7 assistance center"? I know that you answered this question already. However, your answer was to avoid that type of phrase. In my case, I work for a company in which the possessive phrase, which gets abbreviated, is part of a larger phrase. (The above example is real.) Hence, I need to know what to do if you absolutely have to use this sort of wording.

A. If you can't avoid it, you get to choose. You have the power! Use it well.

....

Q. Is there an acceptable way to form the possessive of words such as *Macy's* and *Sotheby's*? Sometimes rewording to avoid the possessive results in less felicitous writing.

A. Less felicitous than *Sotheby's's*? I don't think so.

Words and Letters

Q. How do you set apart a word as a word in a sentence? As in "We are all aware the word fat could be offensive." Would fat be in quotes, italicized, or just left alone?

A. Words used as words must be set off somehow—otherwise the meaning of the sentence can become ambiguous or even unintentionally funny:

He wrote the essay using fat instead of lard.
It was ironic that the misspelled word was right.
He wrote the essay using *fat* instead of *lard*.
It was ironic that the misspelled word was "right."

Chicago favors italics, but quotation marks are also fine.

....

Q. Many of the products that my company offers employ mid-caps (internal capital letters) as well as partial italics—for example, Customer*Cares*. In 8.153, I see that Chicago style is to preserve midcaps in company or product names—do you recommend the same for italics?

A. No, we don't. Once you start trying to accommodate typographic styles, it's hard to stop. There are companies that use bold font or small caps or a backward *R*—and how about those logos where the first letter is small and then the letters get progressively larger, or where the letters have little wings on them? Better to look the other way.

....

Q. With Greek, Arabic, Hebrew, and other non-Latin scripts, should one still italicize words used as words, per 7.58? This comes up a lot in the material I edit. Since the point of italics is to indicate that the word is foreign, does the fact of the non-Latin script accomplish that, thus making italics unnecessary? I had thought so, but then I queried my fellow editors, and many of them seemed to think italics should still be used.

A. You are right: a non-Latin script signals well enough that a language isn't English, so italics aren't needed.

....

Q. The author enclosed the translation of a name in both quotation marks and parentheses. I removed the quotation marks and left just the parentheses. Are both types of punctuation needed? What is the best way to handle this? Example: The Foreign Name ("translated name") blah blah . . .

A. If the foreign name is a proper name (an organization, a building, a place), you don't need quotation marks: Il Popolo della Libertà (The People of Freedom); la mer Rouge (the Red Sea). If the foreign word is a term or concept, you can quote or not, as you please: *lavoro* ("work"), or *lavoro* (work); *CMOS* 13.73 favors parentheses without quotation marks. Foreign titles of published works are formatted like English titles.

....

Q. Is it the three R's or Rs? The *NYT* seems to use R's—I thought I'd double check with you folks before I publish something.

A. Either way is fine, but Chicago style is Rs. (The *New York Times* evidently prefers to follow *NYT* style.) Please see *CMOS* 7.14.

CHAPTER TWO

"'President of the Mess Hall' is going to look pretty silly"

Capitalization can be confounding, as the questions below will attest. Not only are there fashions and trends (remember Truth and Beauty?), but dictionaries and style guides disagree over whether and when to cap.

CMOS to the rescue! Editors usually follow a style manual for help with capping, and Chicago has plenty of advice on the subject. We're admittedly a little offbeat in our "down" style—that is, we prefer to lowercase whenever possible, even in some cases where few others would. It's just part of what makes us special.

Proper Nouns

Q. The *CMOS* rules (8.21) point to "secretary of state" but "Secretary of State Clinton" or "Secretary Clinton," so I am using "president" but "President Kirchner." But shouldn't I capitalize "the Pinochet Dictatorship"? and what about "the Kirchner Administration" and "the Kirchner Government"? Rather than "generic terms associated with governmental bodies" (8.64), they all form an important part of recent Latin American history, like the Mexican Revolution. In addition, they "follow a name and are used as an accepted part of the name" (8.50).

A. While *administration* and *government* are commonly capped in sources that don't follow *CMOS*, to my eye "the Pinochet Dictatorship" (capped) looks bizarre. Can you imagine it stamped at the top of letterhead stationery or etched in gold leaf on a door? If so, then go ahead and cap it (even though Chicago wouldn't).

....

Q. When writing out a person's title that includes a hyphen, when the first letter would be capitalized, should the word following the hyphen also be capitalized (e.g., Co-Founder)?

A. No. In Chicago style, the second half of a hyphenated word that begins with a prefix is lowercased, although there are exceptions. Please see *CMOS* 8.159, point 3. Note too that Chicago does not hyphenate *co-* words (*CMOS* 7.85, section 4).

....

Q. When should the word *century* be capitalized? I know it would not be capitalized in this case: "It's not happened in this century." But what about this: "Were many people rich in the eighteenth century?" or "What did people wear in eighteenth-century Pennsylvania?"

A. Chicago style treats *century* like *day, month,* or *year*; we would lowercase it in all the contexts you cite.

Q. Can you revisit the issue of capitalization of *city of* and *state of* when used to identify an employer? Under 7.40 in the 14th edition, words such as *city* and *state* "are capitalized when they are used as an accepted part of the proper name." Presumably you mean accepted by the powers of *CMOS*. In my example, Jan Johnson works for the (c)ity of Johnsonville, and I would like to offer her recognition in a conference brochure along with Rick Ricker of the state department of transportation. Suffice to say that heated debate is generated when one questions the way things always have been done.

A. Although Chicago editors were willing to travel personally to every burg in America to determine their accepted names, unfortunately the university wouldn't fund us. Instead, we were forced to revise *CMOS* to include the following in the 15th edition (at 8.56): "Governmental entities: Where the government rather than the place is meant, the words *state*, *city*, and the like are usually capitalized." I hope this allows you to recognize everyone with full capitalization honors.

....

Q. Combining 8.21 or 8.22 with 8.32 in the 16th edition suggests that you would condone these sentences: "The queen had tea with the Queen Mother." "The president and the First Lady waved to the crowd." Is that a correct interpretation of Chicago style?

A. Not exactly. Rather, *CMOS* encourages users to apply its guidelines with flexibility and common sense. When rules bump up against each other, try to think like an editor. "First Lady" is conventionally capped as an honorific because its meaning isn't always clear if it's lowercased: In line at the theater, the first lady was wearing no coat. (Who was coatless, the president's wife or the woman standing first in line?) In your sentence, paired with "the president," "first lady" may be safely lowercased, since confusion is unlikely. In your paired examples, treat both titles the same, whichever style you choose.

....

Q. Every institution for which I have worked seems to have a different practice relating to the capitalization of *college* or *university* when referring to the specific institution while dropping the proper name. I used to work for Cornell University's admissions office. That office insisted on not capitalizing *university* when using the word without *Cornell* but still referring to CU specifically. For example,

Once I visited Cornell, there was no choice left for me to make. I fell in love with the university—the people were so friendly and helpful. It didn't hurt that the campus was gorgeous either!

I had previously been told that one should capitalize *university* or *college* when referring to a specific institution. If Cornell's practice is correct, could you please explain why?

A. Cornell's practice strictly follows the recommendations set forth in *The Chicago Manual of Style*. Most institutions (including the University of Chicago itself) do not follow our rule, however. The purpose of a university's literature about itself is to promote itself. Each university is, to itself, the only University in the entire world that matters. That's fine. The recommendations in *CMOS* are intended to promote objective analytical writing—a mission that's not always convenient in promotional settings. But maybe more universities (including ours) should follow the example of Cornell—especially if they want to attract more prospective copyeditors.

....

Q. I doubt I will have the power to change this, but coworkers have insisted that common nouns like *incidents* and *requests* be capitalized in all communications because they are capitalized in the original contract. So folks are to "report Incidents or submit Requests," and "high-priority Incidents" must be reported a certain way. I think the capitalization is unnecessary. Is it correct? I really just want personal and internal vindication, but I'd accept being corrected.

A. Although common nouns should be lowercased in a term paper or newspaper article or book or any other kind of formal writing, if people want certain words to pop in internal office memos or advertisements, capping is a way to achieve that. Legal documents require caps for defined terms, so if you're working in a law office, you might ask a higher-up the reason for capitals, and then do as you're told. (And if you grew up reading the original *Winnie-the-Pooh* books, you can enjoy a secret chuckle at the pomposity the capitals convey, here as there.)

....

Q. Hi, Chicago editors. Three of our editors have a question about capitalization of certain military terms: special ops, officers' mess hall, president of the mess hall. Two of us believe they should all be lowercase—as should American embassy and/or consulate. Thanks for your help.

A. Chicago style is to lowercase all of these, although looking at *CMOS* 8.111, you might argue for capping Special Ops in some contexts. Likewise, American Embassy would not look odd in many documents. If you're following Chicago and not capping the pope or the queen, however, "President of the Mess Hall" is going to look pretty silly.

....

Q. For front matter, we have eleven or twelve endorsements from prominent deans, presidents, and directors of various international programs. I realize that we generally leave those titles lowercased unless we're talking about a Named Chair of So and So, but this one is killing me: Senior Fellow at the Blah-Blah Institute. Should I lowercase "senior fellow"?

A. Are you afraid readers will read "senior fellow" as "old guy"? If so, you had better cap it.

....

Q. Section 8.52 has Illinois and Chicago Rivers (uppercase *R*). Section 8.55 has Fifty-Seventh and Fifty-Fifth Streets (uppercase *S*). Section 8.65 has Communist parties (lowercase *p*). The third seems illogical. Are you contemplating changing?

A. If you look closely, you will see that the third example is not the same. The first two examples are of two proper names that have been amalgamated into a single reference: Illinois River (capped) and Chicago River (capped). "Communist parties" does not refer to the Communist Party and the Communist Party, but to unnamed (and lowercased) parties that are Communist in nature. It's possible that these parties don't even have the word "Communist" or "Party" in their names, so it would be both illogical and misleading to cap *parties* in this case. It would make sense, however, to cap "Republican and Democratic Parties."

....

Q. If *etc.* falls at the end of a title of a work, should it be capitalized or left lowercased? The argument against capitalization is that the *et* part of the abbreviation is a conjunction and the *c* part represents the final word (*cetera*). No one here argues for *etC.*, of course, but my argument is that once *et cetera* is abbreviated to *etc.* the two words become one, so that *etc.* is therefore the last word, not the last two words, in the headline or title, and that it should be capitalized as *Etc.*

A. I like your reasoning, especially if the word is important to the title: *Murder, Etc.* On the other hand, by reversing your logic you might get away with lowercasing when *etc.* is an insignificant, tacked-on ending (*pace CMOS* 8.157): "Schneeweisschean Applications of Jungian Typologies: Dopey, Happy, Bashful, Grumpy, etc."

....

Q. I see in section 8.21 of the 16th edition that civil titles, such as "secretary of state," should be lowercase unless appearing as, for example, "Secretary of State Smith." What about titles such as "assistant secretary of state for bureaucracy and obfuscation"? Should "bureaucracy and obfuscation" be lowercase to match "assistant secretary of state" or should it be capitalized as the name of a specific department?

A. Chicago style lowercases the title of the person but uppercases the department name: "Jordan Smith is assistant secretary of bureaucracy and obfuscation." "The Department of Bureaucracy and Obfuscation requires advance notice of emergency absences." "Anyone who works for Bureaucracy and Obfuscation should keep her résumé up to date."

....

Q. How is capitalization handled in questions of ambiguous geographical origin? I'm trying to rationalize 8.37 and 8.60. Is it "German shepherd," on the grounds that the term refers to the putative geographical origin of the dog, or "german shepherd," in the same way that you have "swiss cheese" and "french dressing" on the grounds that the term is nonliteral, meant to evoke recall of a geographic place irrespective of the actual origin? (If this is confusing because German shepherds may originate from Germany, what about Australian shepherds, which have nothing to do with Australia whatsoever?)

A. *CMOS* can list only so many examples, and it's no good wasting time pondering fine distinctions, so if your document uses some terms that Chicago lowercases and others you aren't sure about, rather than agonize over possible inconsistencies, just look up the words in a dictionary: *CMOS* lowercases french dressing and swiss cheese, but *Merriam-Webster's Collegiate Dictionary* (11th ed.) uppercases them (along with Australian shepherd and German shepherd). Make your choices with a view to minimizing inconsistencies, and record them in your style sheet.

Titles of Works

Q. Can you please confirm the correct spelling of *TIME* magazine? *CMOS* 8.169 has *Time* magazine. However, TIME customer service tells me that *TIME Magazine* is correct. I think *magazine* should be lowercased, since it does not appear anywhere on the cover, and I do not think it is part of the official name of the magazine, even though they capitalize it on their website. What do you think?

A. We're sticking with *Time* magazine. One of the best things about having a style guide is not having to phone every organization in a document and talk to customer service; instead, we use the style manual to present titles consistently. Even if you were to check the periodical itself, you might find that the magazine cover has one spelling (*TIME*) but the copyright information has another (Time) and yet another is used in running text (*Time*). And you know for sure that if you phoned again, a different rep would give you a different answer.

....

Q. I'm confused about what to do when shortening the titles of books. The author refers to *Alice's Adventures in Wonderland* as *Alice in Wonderland*, and I think that it should remain italicized. In addition, there is a dialogue in which a character asks, "Do you remember in *Harry Potter*, when the students are walking up the stairs?" I also think this should be italicized, but I can't find an answer.

A. If a phrase is part of a book title, make it italic. This lets readers know you're referring to a book (or movie, which we also italicize) rather than a person or place. In the case of *Harry Potter*, there's a whole series of books, and Chicago style puts series titles in roman type: the Harry Potter series. This means that in some contexts it won't really matter whether you use italics or not, since either meaning (book or series) will do. It also means that sometimes you'll want to be a little more specific: "Do you remember in *Harry Potter and the Goblet of Fire*, when the students are walking up the stairs?"

....

Q. A coworker with a PhD in English lit comments that your example of title casing "Four Theories concerning the Gospel according to Matthew" isn't correct at all. *Concerning* and *according* are participles, not prepositions (thus these are participial, not prepositional, phrases). I've absolutely never seen "Gospel according to Anyone"—it's always "According to." Thoughts? I'm not just nitpicking; trying to get a group of proofreaders and editors to pull together consistently on little stuff like this.

A. Gulp—a PhD in English lit? Well, here goes: Although *concerning* and *according* are participles, that doesn't stop them from forming prepositions. (You can confirm this in a dictionary.) In the title cited, *concerning* is a preposition with the object *Gospel*, and *according to* is a preposition with the object *Matthew*, so according to Chicago style they are lowercased. Many publishers follow a different guideline for title casing, however, by which all words over a certain length are uppercased, so it's not surprising if you see these prepositions uppercased in titles.

Q. Should the word *nature* be capitalized in this sentence? "My research goal is to advance a global energy solution copied from Nature itself: artificial photosynthesis."

A. If you want the reader to picture a goddess dressed in a flowing garment and flinging fruit and flowers everywhere, yes, cap it and change *itself* to *herself*. Otherwise, no.

CHAPTER THREE

"Three people have three strong opinions about commas . . ."

Many people write to the Chicago Q&A hoping that we can settle a disagreement. "My author [boss, wife, etc.] insists" is a common opener. We're constantly taken aback by how much havoc a tiny comma can wreak in a document—not to mention in a relationship.

But that's what happens when there's more than one way to skin a sentence. Not just commas, but hyphens, bullets, dashes, ellipses—all need wrangling according to some method or other. And in the process, we've found, even punctuation can be taken personally.

Commas

Q. I usually put a comma in the opening salutation of an e-mail— "Hi, Megan"—and this always pleases Megan, a journalist, who believes e-mail salutations should follow the rules of dialogue punctuation. But when I write to Ruth, a physical therapist, I revert to "Hi Ruth," honoring Ruth's opinion that a comma after "Hi" in an e-mail looks nerdy. Are Megan and I correct? Is Ruth on to something? Valuing my friendship with each, should I continue to respect the opinions of both?

A. Your question sent the team here into a dithering frenzy. After several meetings and polls, however, the decision is in: you and Megan are a good match, but you should probably let your friendship with Ruth fade. (The punctuation, for e-mailing purposes, is moot.)

....

Q. We use CMOS 14 and can find no solution to the following problem. "When we first met, he had done the unforgivable, and it had come out so naturally I'd been pleased rather than offended." It seems the comma before *and* is unnecessary. Our author disagrees. Can you help?

A. I'm sorry I can't check the 14th edition for you; I sold my copy to an antique collector after I tried to donate it to a home for retired copyeditors and nobody wanted it (they all had the 16th). CMOS 16 (6.28) is very helpful on the subject, however, recommending a comma in that position.

....

Q. My editor and I disagree about comma placement in this sentence. I added the comma, but he says it's not necessary. Your opinion, please? "The screen design includes functional elements like text-entry boxes and list boxes, and stylistic elements like graphics and multimedia." Thanks!

A. Your editor objects because it's a "rule" not to put a comma between two elements making up a compound object.

The comma is needed in your sentence, however, because your two elements are themselves compound. Without the comma, the reader is left to navigate some pretty rickety syntax: X includes A like B and C and D like E and F. Readability trumps the rule, so the comma should stay.

....

Q. I have been debating with my copyeditor guidelines concerning commas and dates. We consulted 6.45 on the topic but we still differ in opinion. I prefer "In the summer of 1812 General Hagerthy moved his troops" versus "In the summer of 1812, General Hagerthy moved his troops." "Early in 1946 an opportunity came for my cousin" versus "Early in 1946, an opportunity came for my cousin." I argue that a comma after the year is not needed. Gurus of style, please opine who is correct.

A. Rejoice: everyone is correct. Higher authorities are not interested in legislating commas to this degree. Peace.

....

Q. A physicists' society newsletter reported on some portraits by famed physicist and part-time artist Richard Feynman, noting, "The works were acquired by Princeton, where Feynman had been a graduate student, in the mid-eighties." One reader chided the editors, claiming that the sentence makes Feynman (born 1918) a sixty-plus-year-old graduate student. I feel the comma after "graduate student" sets off the phrase correctly. How do I make my case concisely, or what rule do I cite? Or am I wrong?

A. Bad writing can be technically correct. In this case, citing a punctuation rule to justify the word order can't save the sentence from its comical implication. Why force readers to analyze the commas in order to ascertain the meaning of a sentence? Good editing smooths the way for the reader. Good editing would move "in the mid-eighties" to follow "acquired." In that light, I'm afraid you are wrong.

....

Q. Three people have three strong opinions about commas in the following passage: "He thinks that, if he asks for directions, his membership in the brotherhood of men will be revoked. He would rather be lost." Person A likes both commas. Person B would omit the first but keep the second. Person C would strike both. Please judge us.

A. Group hug! You are all correct. Person A's version is the least elegant to my ear, but it's not wrong. Please see *CMOS* 6.32.

Hyphens

Q. I tend to let my ear be my guide—and usually that works—so I need some clarification to ensure I'm on the right track. Can you clarify that I am using my hyphens correctly? Facilitate a core-team workshop to discuss . . . Develop a future-state document . . . Conduct a future-state assessment . . . Identify change-management opportunities.

A. Maybe it's time for a Q-tip. This kind of business-speak can become a habit to the point where you no longer hear the ambiguities. Is a "future-state document" about the future of your state or the state of the future? Are change-management opportunities about changing management or managing change? Hyphenation should be a last resort. Instead, try writing in more natural English: Facilitate a workshop where the core team will discuss . . . Develop a document that looks ahead . . . Assess the future of . . . Identify opportunities to manage change.

....

Q. I am editing a magazine article related to real estate and am struggling with how to hyphenate the descriptions. "With seven bedrooms, four full and two half bathrooms, this home has 6,000 square feet of living space." Also, "This is a 2,000 square foot, fully renovated four bedroom, three and a half bathroom home." What does *CMOS* suggest?

A. Thank you for asking! Reading real estate ads can be painful for us. Your first sentence is passable; the second one needs a lot of hyphens. Please refer to many such examples in the hyphenation table at *CMOS* 7.85. If a compound phrase (number + noun) serves as an adjective and comes before the noun it modifies, it usually needs hyphens:

a three-and-a-half-bathroom home
a four-bedroom townhouse
a 600-square-foot studio
a 2,000-square-foot, fully renovated four-bedroom, three-and-a-
    half-bathroom home

If the compound phrase (number + noun) serves as a noun itself and does not modify a noun that follows, it does not need hyphens:

a home with three and a half bathrooms
a townhouse with four bedrooms
a studio of 600 square feet

a home with seven bedrooms, four full and two half bathrooms, and 6,000 square feet of living space

....

Q. My staff and I encountered a phrase and there's a bit of debate as to how to hyphenate it: Wall Street darling-ready. Some believe an en dash should be inserted between *Street* and *darling*, followed by the hyphen between *darling* and *ready*. Others, however, feel the addition of the en dash would make the phrase even more difficult to interpret for readers. Thoughts?

A. I'm sorry, but the phrase looks like nonsense; I don't think you can save it by tacking on hyphens or dashes. Please rewrite the sentence and—as they say—murder your darling.

....

Q. My understanding is that the word *family* is a noun or adjective. So if you use it in a sentence like "We ordered a family-sized pizza for the party," is the hyphen used correctly in this instance despite the fact *family* ends in *ly*?

A. When *CMOS* 5.91 says "A two-word phrasal adjective that begins with an adverb ending in *-ly* is not hyphenated," it's referring to adverbs (not nouns or adjectives) where *-ly* is added to a root word: *slyly, gladly*. Words like *ply, homily*, and *family* happen to end in *-ly*, but the *-ly* is not an ending; it's part of the word. And they aren't adverbs. The section of the hyphenation table (*CMOS* 7.85) that you're looking for is "noun + participle" (*family* + *sized*), where you will see that the hyphen is correct.

....

Q. In a technical proposal, would you say "400-ton-per-day scrubber" or "400-tons-per-day scrubber"? Thanks a bunch!

A. The first construction is the more usual one. (Btw, what *is* a 400-ton-per-day scrubber, exactly? And where can we get one?)

....

Q. I'm editing a report about the EPA's Climate Ready Estuaries program. Unfortunately, the program's formal name has no hyphen, but there are several instances of "climate ready" as a phrasal adjective throughout the paper. I obviously can't insert a hyphen into the program name, and I'm naturally averse to leaving "climate ready" unhyphenated. But this creates at least the appearance of inconsistency. What's a diligent hyphenator to do?

A. The hyphenator needs to chill. Proper names and titles are allowed to diverge from style, and there's no shame in that. If the text is consistent within itself, you've done your job. If the apparent inconsistency really bothers you, the obvious remedy is to break style and leave the phrase unhyphenated everywhere.

....

Q. Should "64 Slice Cardiac Computed Tomography Angiography Program" be hyphenated "64-Slice"?

A. Yes, hyphenate. (Sounds messy. Any chance you're in the market for a lightly used 400-ton-per-day scrubber?)

Vertical Lists and Bullets

Q. Is it ever okay to start a list with a sentence ending in a period instead of a colon? ("To determine the answer, use the following concepts.") Does it matter if the list is set off by bullets or that the typesetting is different (by color or font, etc.)? What is the preferred method if both ways are correct? What if it is not a complete sentence? I appreciate the response. Me and a fellow copy editor are at odds.

A. Chicago's preference is to use a colon, but there are times when a period might better serve. Please see *CMOS* 6.124–26 for details on how to punctuate vertical lists and for examples that include sentences and sentence fragments. If you use a period, the list items should begin with capital letters. (P.S. I am averting my eyes from "Me and a fellow copy editor are at odds"—please tell me that this is just your fun e-mail-writing style, or if it isn't, that you aren't editing anything important to our national security.)

....

Q. In either numbered or bulleted vertical lists, what is the correct syntax? Should each item begin the same way—for example, with a verb?

A. Various syntaxes work well (sentences, fragments, questions), but when the items are parallel in syntax, it creates an order and logic that helps readers take in information more easily than a mixture of constructions. Parallel doesn't mean identical, however. If your items are complex, it may not be practical to match them word for word with parallel parts of speech. On the other hand, in a simple construction, close imitation is usually easy and effective. (If your first two items are "Stop" and "Drop," you aren't going to follow with "How to roll around when you're on fire.")

Q. In a list of bulleted points where some are complete sentences and some are not, do you put a period at the end of a sentence, but not the list, or periods after all bulleted points, or none at all?

A. I'm afraid you won't like my answer: this situation is not covered in *CMOS* because in a list of bulleted points all the items should be styled with the same syntax, either sentences or sentence fragments.

....

Q. I do not believe it makes sense to use a bulleted list of one item. If it is just one item, should it not simply be a paragraph? At the end of many of our sections in an advocacy guide we have "Advocacy Reminders." Sometimes there are many; sometimes there is only one reminder. It seems to me if there is one reminder it should be a paragraph.

A. Although logically a list should have more than one item, bullets are more forgiving, especially if throughout a book like yours, reminders are formatted in a special section the same way in every chapter. The visual cue of the identical formatting would override a quibble about the logic of a single bullet point. Your bullets can be considered more like decorations than hierarchy markers.

Other Dots, Dashes, and Squiggles

Q. When using an en dash to indicate a range of time, is it wrong to use *from* in front of the time range (from 9am–5pm)?

A. Although most readers will know what you mean by it, "from 9–5" is inelegant because it uses a spelled-out word for the *from* part of the expression and lets a symbol (the en dash) take the place of the *to* part of the expression. The reader is left hanging, waiting for the spelled-out *to* part, as in "We work a variety of shifts, anywhere *from* 9–5 *to* 11–3." Or "Several age ranges were surveyed, *from* 5–10 *to* 70–75." If you want to use *from* with 9–5, make the *to* explicit: We work from 9 to 5. Otherwise omit *from*: We work 9–5.

....

Q. Dear *CMS*, I am nearly done revising my dissertation, but my advisor may not pass me on account of my lengthy em dashes! I am using Times New Roman, and apparently the em dashes are too long. Is the standard em dash in Times acceptable for thesis publication? If so, can I point my advisor to something in the *CMS* on this? (I am serious. I don't think she would not pass me, but she has circled every em dash and said, "Too long. Fix!" on my drafts, and I'd like not to chance it.)

A. Well, that's pretty crazy. For publication, it makes no difference what font is in the manuscript—typesetters follow the publisher's specs—but it looks as though you might have to change the font for your dissertation. Palatino has shorter em dashes than Times New Roman. If you are required to use Times New Roman, change only the dashes to Palatino and maybe no one will notice. You can make a global replacement. Good luck!

Q. Is it appropriate to add a semicolon before *i.e.* or *e.g.*? For example, is it correct to say "by focusing on prevention; i.e., identifying and intervening"?

A. You can use a comma unless the material after the abbreviation starts a new independent clause.

> She carried only the essentials, i.e., business cards, lipstick, pepper spray.
>
> She saw to the last two details; i.e., flowers were waiting and the driver kept mum.

In either case a colon, an em dash, or parentheses might also work. And please note that Chicago doesn't use *i.e.* or *e.g.* in running text (though we allow them in parentheses or notes). Instead we use *that is* or a similar phrase. In many sentences, you don't really need the abbreviation; a colon or dash alone would be better.

....

Q. I have written a novel and am currently working with an editor, and we have different attitudes toward the use of the semicolon. According to my editor I have used semicolons copiously, but I have done so in order to achieve the connection of thoughts and ideas that are related but not so closely that they require a comma, and in order to avoid a series of the staccatolike sentences that so much current literature is subject to. Is this acceptable in today's modern fiction?

A. Although an editor should respect a writer's voice and style, a writer doesn't always realize how her voice comes across after it passes through the wickets of punctuation. There should be collaboration here. Your editor should consider each semicolon before nixing it, rather than wipe them all out on principle alone. You should acknowledge that a surfeit of semicolons can distract any reader who sees it as a writing tic; it can also be unsightly on the page, depending on the typeface. Here's an idea: Find a passage where semicolons dominate and ask someone to read it out loud. Then replace the semicolons with commas or periods and ask someone else to read it to you. See whether you hear a difference. It might help you determine the best course.

....

Q. Hi there! For a sign for bachelorette parties, would the phrase "Bachelorette Out of Control" be more appropriate than "Bachelorette's Out of Control"? The question is one of contraction, because I don't see how "Bachelorette's Out of Control" can be correct without "The" prefacing it. Thank you!

A. Out-of-control bachelorettes who require appropriate signage aren't very convincing, but the first version is better.

....

Q. In a sentence, a colon should always be preceded by an independent clause. Why doesn't the *Chicago Manual* state this explicitly? All your examples follow the principle. Why doesn't the manual just say that the introductory clause has to be independent?

A. Because we're a bunch of spineless and ineffectual prevaricators? Or because there are times when a colon need not be preceded by an independent clause? A case in point: this one.

Q. In the sentence "The times, they are a changin'" does the period come before or after the apostrophe? Logic would dictate after, but it does not look right aesthetically.

A. Logic wins in this case: the apostrophe is part of the word, not punctuation for the sentence, and therefore it must cleave to the word, ugly or not: changin'.

....

Q. I've read 13.48 et seq., but I want to verify that what you're recommending is [space dot space dot space dot space] for a regular ellipsis. Also, I am puzzled by the rationale of putting a period at the end of an incomplete sentence and then an ellipsis before continuing the quotation. As I see it, this doesn't differentiate between a complete sentence followed by missing text and an incomplete sentence followed by missing text.

A. You are right; the traditional system does not distinguish between a complete sentence followed by missing text at the beginning of the next sentence, and an incomplete sentence followed by the intact beginning of the next sentence. The period merely indicates that the two chunks of text belong to different sentences. If it's important to distinguish, then you must format the passage as two separate quotations. Please note, too, that we add a period only at the end of an independent clause.

....

Q. Is there a period after an abbreviation of a country if it is terminating a sentence? "I went to the U.K.."

A. Seriously, have you ever seen two periods in a row like that in print? If we told you to put two periods, would you do it? Would you set your hair on fire if *CMOS* said you should?

CHAPTER FOUR

"Can *fewest* mean zero?"

USE OR ABUSE? * RESTRICTION *
GENDER BENDERS * PREPOSITIONS * PRONOUNS *
GRAMMATICAL OR NOT?

Grammar and style can be tricky. Editors who make a career out of understanding them can become just as confused as the next Joe when the language catches us off guard. Sometimes not even a grammar book or style guide can lead us from the wilderness. This is when we turn to usage manuals and dictionaries for additional help.

Usage is a category that overlaps with grammar but slides into grayer areas involving regionalisms, jargon, and nonstandard forms of English. Sometimes, sorting out acceptable grammar and usage calls for more than a reference book. Sometimes, we actually have to . . . think.

Use or Abuse?

Q. Can *fewest* mean zero? Example: Which desk has the fewest books? If one desk has no books, does that desk contain the fewest? Or must *fewest* refer to a number (however small) that is greater than zero?

A. Think about the desk. If it doesn't have more books than the other desks, and it doesn't have the same number of books, what's left? It must have the fewest. But if several desks have no books, then our desk does not have the fewest, and it's clearer to say that it has no books. (Was that a trick question?)

....

Q. A friend and I are disagreeing about the following phrases: "less and less likely" versus "more and more unlikely." I say they are equal in meaning. He says that only the first one is correct. Your opinion, please.

A. My opinion is that your friend should be asked to supply justification or proof. (Don't worry—he won't be able to.)

....

Q. Do you have a problem (as I do) with the phrase "the fact that," and if so, what alternatives do you offer?

A. In spite of its banishment from style guides (probably thanks to Messrs. Strunk and White), the phrase sometimes has useful meaning. Where it's redundant or overused, it should be edited out, but if it's doing honest work, there's no reason to be offended by it. Arthur Plotnik quotes the following from Don DeLillo's *Underworld*: "Sister Grace believed the proof of God's creativity eddied from the fact that you could not surmise the life, even remotely, of his humblest shut-in." I wouldn't mess with that, would you?

....

Q. I often find myself with questions about verb tense in indirect speech. When the main verb is in the past tense (e.g., *said, ar-*

gued), should subordinate verbs also be shifted into the past? For example, in the sentence "Military supporters claimed that the purpose of a nation's standing army is to fight wars, not keep the peace," I am inclined to change *is* to *was*. A cursory web search reveals that "backshifting" is a hotly debated question; does Chicago have a position on it?

A. We don't have a position on it, because writers must be free to use the tense that their meaning requires. You could make a rule that the past must always be used, but that would result in universal ambiguity: "They pointed out that as humans we were fallible" leaves open to question whether we still are. The present tense in "They pointed out that as humans we are fallible" more clearly implies that humans are still fallible today. To restrict writers with an arbitrary rule in this case is not in the interest of clarity.

....

Q. Dear Sir or Madam, I am taking a course on Hispanic linguistics. As part of a project that has been assigned by my professor, I just learned that there is an institution that regulates the usage of the English language (in the United States? Great Britain?). I would like to read more about it. It is my impression that *The Chicago Manual of Style* has part of the job of regulator of the English language. Is this true?

A. If only! But no—there is no institution that can regulate language in the United States or Great Britain, although there are organizations that sometimes pretend to. In both countries people are free to speak and write as they wish. *The Chicago Manual of Style* is a guide for writers who want to write in standard English and use a standard citation format. You can start your research by reading about "language regulators" at Wikipedia.

....

Q. Is it "happy medium" or "happy median"? The author writes: "We would all be much better served as stewards of finite public funds if we could find that happy median where trust reigns supreme." Thanks!

A. The idiom is "happy medium," but I like the image of commuters taking refuge from road rage on the happy median.

....

Q. Is the following correct? "In one of my more popular poems . . ." Is there a hard-and-fast rule regarding *most* versus *more*?

A. Absolutely. In contexts like these, *more* is an unspecified but nonetheless greater quantity than *less*, as well as a possibly exact but unexpressed quantity less than *most*. Of course, if you have a more popular poem, you probably also have a less popular one, so perhaps it's best not to say.

Restriction

Q. I write professional résumés, and I have a question about the use of a comma in a sentence with *including*. My proofer has begun inserting a comma prior to *including* followed by a list: "Managed a variety of projects, including joint, combined, and contingency exercises." Should this comma be omitted?

A. Many readers write to ask whether the word *including* always requires a comma in front of it, but there's no simple answer. Each instance must be decided individually, because a comma changes the meaning.

I invited all the clubs including biker chicks and pit tootsies.
I invited all the clubs, including biker chicks and pit tootsies.

The first sentence is ambiguous; it might mean that I invited only clubs that include biker chicks and pit tootsies among their members. The second sentence makes clear that I invited all clubs, regardless of membership, and that this included the chicks' and tootsies' clubs. In your text you need a comma if the chunk after *including* is nonrestrictive (that is, if some of the projects included joint exercises, some included combined, some both, etc.). Without a comma, *including* becomes restrictive, and the implication is that every project included joint, combined, and contingency exercises.

....

Q. I can't wrap my brain around this question re appositives. In the following sentence, is the man's name restrictive or nonrestrictive? Ask Ruth's childhood friend Tom Jones to help.

A. Unfortunately, it's ambiguous. It used to be that a lack of commas signaled restriction: that is, the meaning of *friend* in your sentence would be restricted to Tom Jones, implying that Ruth had other friends as well. Commas (Ask Ruth's childhood friend, Tom Jones, to help) signaled nonrestriction: that Tom Jones was Ruth's only childhood friend, so his actual name is ancillary, disposable information. It was a pretty good system. Nowadays, however, commas in nonrestrictive constructions have become optional, which is fine when the most likely meaning is obvious (as in "my wife Georgia") but unhelpful in a sentence like yours. And writers everywhere add commas where they aren't needed (Astronaut, Neil Armstrong, waved to the crowd), which adds to the confusion.

....

Q. If you write "In the opening of Raymond Chandler's 1940 novel *Farewell, My Lovely* . . . ," ought there to be a comma after *novel*, as it was his only novel published that year and so what follows is a nonrestrictive appositive? Or does that seem too clunky?

A. The comma is correct, but it can be considered optional in contexts where a writer isn't necessarily privy to the facts that would determine restriction, and where, as you point out, the extra comma would be awkward.

....

Q. I'm troubled by the growing use of syntax such as "The writer William Styron lived in Paris." My suggestion is that Mr. Styron was likely to have had many roles in life but that the sentence structure indicates him to have been only a writer. This first became noticeable in the *New York Times* and later in the *New Yorker* and now elsewhere. I would be comfortable with "William Styron, the writer, went shopping." To my eyes, that is less restrictive of his lifestyle because, for example, we know that whatever he did, he also shopped.

A. You should use the syntax that troubles you the least. (I myself would feel more comfortable knowing that he also took vitamins and brushed his teeth.)

Q. In the following sentence, it would appear that naming Fred as my brother is a nonrestrictive parenthetical: My brother, Fred, and I teach at the same school. However, these commas could be taken as serial commas (my brother and Fred and I teach at the same school). Thus, I was taught to write such a sentence as follows: My brother Fred and I teach at the same school. Which would you consider correct?

A. The clear one is the correct one.

Gender Benders

Q. I'm editing a translation of an ancient Chinese text, the Dao De Jing, which is largely concerned with describing the ideal "Daoist sage ruler." The translator has chosen to use the generic masculine pronoun because in the historical context of the text, rulers were exclusively men. (For instance, "Of the best of all rulers, people will only know that he exists.") I'm inclined to accept this argument, but should I be concerned about gender bias?

A. Although most of us are rooting against gender bias, it probably doesn't help to write it out of our history. If you're concerned about the effect the language will have on impressionable readers, work with the translator to include a note about gender issues in that historical context.

....

Q. I'm in a quandary regarding gender pronouns. In an economics paper (on first-price auctions) that I am editing, the author has defined the actors in his proposition like this: "The female and male pronouns are used for weak and strong bidders, respectively." Is there any exception where gender-biased language is allowed for ease of expression? What do you recommend?

A. You could ask the author whether this usage is conventional in his topic area, but regardless, you should point out that the implication would offend some readers. Suggest that he rethink his shorthand.

....

Q. An author has insisted on placing a *sic* after quoting authors who use *him* or *himself* to refer in general to persons rather than using gender-inclusive language. We think this is a bit pretentious and that the quoted material should stand on its own. Do the wise editors have any advice?

A. The wise editors agree. *Sic* is used to clarify that an error appeared in the original and was not introduced by the writer quoting it. No one reading *him* or *himself* would think it was a typo. Please see *CMOS* 13.59.

....

Q. Can we now use the pronoun *who* in reference to animals and things? If so, is this black and white or are there guidelines to follow? Surely, we cannot say, "The vase who was given to me by May," right? In the 15th edition, the rule was clear: "*Who* refers only to a person." However, in the 16th edition, it is now rephrased: "*Who* . . . normally refers to a person." We checked *Webster's* as well, and true enough, they also said that *who* can be used in reference to animals and things.

A. Not much in language usage is black and white. You wouldn't use *who* with a vase, but you might with a talking bird, or a committee, or a spirit, or a source. *CMOS* 15 was a little too strict in its prohibition, and the 16th rectifies that.

....

Q. I have seen some texts using the pronoun *her* to refer to a business: "Apple's profit was high due to her impressive product designs." I would like to learn when I should use the feminine pronoun and when I should avoid it.

A. Use the feminine pronoun when referring to a female person or animal. Avoid using it to refer to a business, a ship, or any nonliving entity—especially in the presence of a female person.

Prepositions

Q. Dear Sir or Madam, I'm having a disagreement with a coworker on a particular subject, and as my *CMOS* is at home, I can't go to it for a ruling. I'm arguing that the prohibition against ending a sentence with a preposition is an invalid injunction—one that often serves to confuse and befuddle the reader by forcing tortured and mangled word placements. She says that the "rule" must be followed. So, is it appropriate to end a sentence with a preposition? Thank you.

A. That old prohibition is what we call a grammar superstition. You will not find it in any authoritative grammar book. Please see *CMOS* 5.176.

Q. Hi there. I have a question regarding the use of double prepositions. Is there a rule against it? I tried to check for rules in *CMOS*, but I didn't see any. I also checked a dictionary, and it says that "off of" is an idiom and is therefore correct.

A. That "off of" is an idiom does not mean it's correct. In fact, it means that caution is required: many idioms are considered slang or informal. *CMOS* guidelines apply to formal speech and writing, and *CMOS* says never to use "off of" (see 5.220, under *off*). There is no rule against double prepositions, however. "I ran out of the house" and "He peered from behind the tree" are perfectly grammatical and idiomatic.

....

Q. In my role as an editor, I frequently face preposition-conjunction combinations such as this: "The analysis assesses the availability of and access to community services." Does this need commas?

A. Commas around the second phrase ("and access to") will indicate that it is somewhat parenthetical, an afterthought, so use them only if that's the writer's intention.

....

Q. Good morning. What is the right preposition after the noun *change*? I thought it was always *in*. However, Cambridge.org gives the following examples:

Let me know if there's any change in the situation.
They've made a lot of changes to the house.

Now, I'm confused. Please enlighten me. Thanks.

A. The difficult thing about English is that there is almost never a single right preposition for any noun:

a change to the house
a change in the situation
a change of heart
a change for the better
a change since yesterday

A linguist might be able to explain why these usages have become conventional and are not interchangeable, but most native speakers of English learn them intuitively, without being able to articulate the reasons. If English isn't your first language, lots of practice reading and listening to English is probably the best way to train your instincts.

Pronouns

Q. I've always thought that when you use *any* as a pronoun it should be treated as singular. But in the following sentences, "Do they all match? Is any missing?" using *is* feels awkward. Does *any* in this case refer to *they* in the previous sentence?

A. Yes, it does. *Any* can be singular or plural (which I'm sure by now you have learned from checking the dictionary you keep at hand): "Have you checked the pizza? Is any missing?" or "Have you checked the Twinkies? Are any missing?" Both are correct (and around here, most likely missing).

Q. I've always thought that to avoid confusion a pronoun should rename the closest noun to it, but an author says "the pronoun *it* is most naturally taken to repeat the subject of the sentence." The pronoun in question renamed a noun that immediately preceded it (not the subject). Is the author correct? Should *it* always refer to the subject rather than to the closest noun or pronoun?

A. "Always"? Of course not. Your author has in mind a sentence where *it* does not refer to the subject and we sense an awkward ambiguity: The money in the pool of blood reddened as it spread. But it's just as easy to write a perfectly clear sentence where *it* does not refer to the subject—or for that matter to the nearest noun: Did you see the eclipse last night when it peaked? Both you and your author would do well to stop searching for a rule to govern all your sentences and simply rephrase if it isn't crystal clear what *it* refers to.

....

Q. Could you please give a definitive answer to the *its* versus *it's* issue? I just came back from a writing conference, and the advice we received was contradictory to everything I was taught previously, as well as contradictory to what I can find online on college websites. Most writer's websites that I've checked out are claiming that the *only* time *its* is written as *it's* would be when the meaning is "it is." What happened to possessive nouns?

A. True, this can be confusing, but possessive pronouns are an exception to the rule that possessives have apostrophes. Possessive pronouns lack apostrophes: *her* glove, *my* glove, *your* glove, *its* glove. Remembering that *its* is a possessive pronoun should help.

....

Q. I'll often hear people say "me and Kathy," not "Kathy and me." Shouldn't *me* come *after* the person's name? "Kathy and me," not "me and Kathy"?

A. Yes. When *me* is used in a compound object, it normally comes last: The message was sent to Kathy and me. There are times when it might be fine to put *me* first, however, such as when I am the primary object and other people are not equally emphasized: The threat was directed at me and everyone I'd been in contact with since that day. If you're talking about a compound subject (as opposed to object), the correct phrase is "Kathy and I": Kathy and I told them. If *me* is used as a subject, it doesn't really matter which way you decide to be wrong.

....

Q. Can I use the first person?

A. Evidently.

Grammatical or Not?

Q. I often have to edit sentences with dangling modifiers—for example, "As a valued supporter, I am pleased to invite you . . ." My go-to improvement is to add *you* into the sentence: "As you are a valued supporter, I am pleased to invite you . . ." That is, until today I received feedback from a higher-up that said it had to be changed, because "you can't change the subject of the sentence from *you* to *I*." Now I'm really confused! Is that a legitimate critique? Should I just rework the entire sentence? Thanks!

A. Although the higher-up botched the grammar critique (you didn't change the subject of the main sentence; it was always *I*), it's clear that your editing was rejected, so yes, you need to try again. For instance, you could move the offending phrase elsewhere ("I am happy to invite you, a valued supporter, . . .") or make it declarative ("You are a valued supporter, and I am happy to invite you . . ."). If your higher-up just can't part with the opening phrase, explain that you would be happy to reword but can't think of a more efficient way to eliminate the dangling modifier. Using the term "dangling modifier" is often enough to frighten someone who doesn't know grammar into complying.

Q. I read a lot and have been working on a novel of my own for a while now. In most of the materials I read the authors use "had had" and "that that" quite often. For example: "He had had the dog for twelve years and everyone knew that that was the real reason he didn't want Animal Control to take it." I doubt there is any actual rule against this, but I find it to be unattractive on a purely aesthetic basis and try to avoid it like the plague when writing. Is there anything to this or am I just weird?

A. As you can see here, correct isn't always pretty. So you aren't weird; you're a writer, and one of the things that makes you a writer is that you're sensitive to ugliness. Once you're sensitive to clichés, you'll be all set.

Q. My friend Ed says that there is a problem with the sentence "An error occurred while processing your request." More specifically, he says that it sounds like the error is processing the request. Do you see what he is talking about? Is this a legitimate criticism? The sentence in question is a common message from computer systems, and when we asked around, no one could see a problem with it. I wondered if there might be some underlying grammatical exception that explained why the message seemed so clear (despite the error Ed perceived). But I guess it is just one of those things that people understand unambiguously because of its context.

A. Ed is right about there being a grammar problem, because there is no word in the sentence that tells *who* is processing, and the best candidate is *error*. Consider this: if you read "A bird sang while flying by your window," you understand it to mean "A bird sang while [it, the bird, was] flying by your window." The grammar is the same in "An error occurred while [it, the error, was] processing your request." It's true that people generally understand this construction from its context without perceiving it as an error. The danger is when language like this is used to dodge responsibility for an action. It's more honest to clean up the grammar and name the actor: "An error occurred while *we were* processing your request.

....

Q. I've encountered a sentence that is giving me more confusion than it should. The sentence in question is this: "Enjoyment is not as an important function for courting as it is for dating." I cannot figure out if it should read "as important a function." I think if I could figure out what grammatical function "as" is serving in this sentence, I could make sense of it, but I have been staring at it long enough to addle my brain.

A. Although your editing will put it right, the "as . . . as" construction (adverb and conjunction, respectively) is not always clear or economical. It would be better to trim and rephrase: "Enjoyment is less important for courting than for dating." (As for the difference between courting and dating and why it's OK for courting to be less fun, I assume you're investigating.)

CHAPTER FIVE

"If you give birth to a source and he's still living under your roof . . ."

....

....

Citing sources for the evidence and quotations contained in a document is a loathsome business, but it has to be done, and it has to be done correctly. Students and scholars tear their hair over quoting correctly—and even more over the meticulous formatting required in notes and bibliographies. Their grades, jobs, and careers can depend on getting it right. *CMOS* devotes two hefty chapters to documenting sources and another one to quotations. But not even *CMOS* could anticipate the growing number and variety of sources writers want to quote and cite when documenting their work.

How Do You Cite . . . ?

Q. How does one cite a food label? My friend is writing her dissertation on the local-food movement and branding (among other things), and she's curious about how to properly cite some labels she's using in her research.

A. There is no particular "proper" way to cite a food label in the sense that a style manual will include an example you can follow. Even so, it's understandable that your friend wants something more scholarly than "I saw this Twinkie label . . ." Following general guidelines for citing, your friend should list whatever will help a reader locate the label to check it personally, such as the brand, the type of food, the type of packaging, the date on the label, or the date observed. There is no point in trying to force the information into a standard note or bibliography citation format. Photos of the labels might be more helpful than pseudocitations.

....

Q. Browsing both the 15th and 16th editions for citation rules, I don't see instruction on how to cite live performance. Given that performance studies, dance/theater criticism, and musicology/ethnomusicology are established disciplines, and that observing live performance is a necessary research method, I don't see why that source (and its creators/producers) should not be cited.

A. It's not that Chicago rejects live performance as a legitimate source; there simply isn't room for examples of every kind. If live performances are the backbone of your research, the lack of a citation form in *CMOS* should not prevent you from citing them. You can mimic the standard order of citation elements (performer, title, place, date) or order them in a way that makes sense for your work, such as chronologically for works by the same person.

Q. Please help. I need to cite a few lines from a poem, but there are no page numbers in the book of poems. Do I make page numbers up? Do I use poem 1, poem 2? My cites are to be author/date style. For example, after my quote I need to reference it, as in (Grimes 1999, ???). No page numbers!

A. If you've already mentioned the poem's title or number, you can write (Grimes 1999, n.p.), which indicates that there are no page numbers. If you haven't mentioned a title or number, you can add it to the citation: (Grimes 1999, "Something Will Happen"). "N.p." is optional in any case.

....

Q. In the citation of the following newspaper showing various issues and page numbers, would it be written like this?

    1. *Southern Patriot*, 20 January 1835, 3, 27 January 1835, 3, 30 January 1835, 3, 2 February 1835, 3, 3 February 1835, 3, 3 March 1835, 3, and 19 March 1835, 3.

A. No. I'm afraid my vision began to blur when I came to "1835, 3, 27." This calls for the deployment of what Lynne Truss calls "a kind of Special Policeman in the event of comma fights," that is, the semicolon (*Eats, Shoots & Leaves* [New York: Gotham Books, 2004], 125):

    1. *Southern Patriot*, 20 January 1835, 3; 27 January 1835, 3; 30 January 1835, 3; 2 February 1835, 3; 3 February 1835, 3; 3 March 1835, 3; and 19 March 1835, 3.

An alternative is to omit the page numbers, as is often done in newspaper citations, since articles may migrate from one page to another in different editions of the same paper.

....

Q. I recently wrote an essay and used some information that my adult son gave me, and when I told him I was using it, he said I had to cite him. In my view, if you give birth to a source and he's still living under your roof, you don't have to cite him. What's your view?

A. I'm sorry, but I'm afraid you do owe him something for the material. If you don't want to credit him in a citation, you might try to cast this as a work-for-hire arrangement. Tell him you'll negotiate the payment the next time you're negotiating his rent.

....

Q. I'm using Shelley Jackson's short story "Skin" as a primary source in an article I'm writing, but the story is published only as tattoos on the bodies of volunteers (one word per volunteer). How do I cite this work?

A. Cite it the same way you would "cite" your sandwich or your miniblinds or the fluff under your bathroom rug—not by trying to pretend it is a bibliographic source, but simply by telling what it is. In the text or in a note, write something like "Shelley Jackson's 'Skin' is a story published only as tattoos on the bodies of volunteers (one word per volunteer)."

Notes

Q. Should *ibid*. in note citations be italicized? Are block quotes always a smaller font size than the rest of the text? If a publisher specifies that only US and not British spelling should be used in a manuscript, should quoted words be changed as well?

A. No. No. No.

....

Q. I need to cite a quotation I took from a text which was originally reproduced in a book ("book 1") that cites the archival source of the text in question. The book I am taking the quotation from cites book 1. How should I cite the quotation? How far should I go in citing, knowing that the original text is an archival document that has been reproduced several times? When citing in footnotes, can I write "Transcribed in . . ."?

A. The more intermediaries between you and the original text, the further you are from actual evidence and the closer to rumor. If you can't consult the original archived document, you owe it to your readers to convey the chain of transmission. It won't necessarily be pretty. "Transcribed in" is a fine way to start.

....

Q. In a footnote I have a quote that, in the original, itself has a footnote. The latter footnote (i.e., the original author's footnote) is salient to the discussion, and I'd like to include it in my footnote. What are the mechanics to handle such a situation? Currently I have this:

1. Author (date: page) writes, "Body of quote [original author's footnote *] ([original author's footnote #] body of footnote)."

A. This seems more complicated than necessary. You could simplify by leaving out the footnote number, which conventionally would be left out in any case (see *CMOS* 13.7). After the close of the text quote, write "Smith adds in a note that . . ." If you like, reference the note number at the end of that quote or paraphrase, e.g., (2004, 25n16).

....

Q. How many works to include in a single citation? The following in-text note citation includes too many works, to my taste: (Hong & Kuo 1999; Holton 2001; Rowden 2001; Reichert 1998; Gravin 1994; Holt et al. 2000; Griego et al. 2000; Thomsen & Hoest 2001; Goh 2003; Porth et al. 1999; Gardiner & Whiting 1997; Watkins & Marsick 1998). Does anyone have a rule that can be helpful in deciding (1) how many works are too many? (2) what you do with the works that have to be deleted? Suggest incorporating them elsewhere?

A. Author-date style can get ugly, and your wish to trim this string is understandable. But the right number of works is however many works the writer needs to list in support of the point she is making. It's not a good idea for an editor to whittle down a writer's documentation. Readers in disciplines that use author-date style are used to being interrupted by it; they seem to appreciate the economical delivery of the information.

....

Q. When can we use *apud* in a note?

A. *Apud* (Latin for "at," "beside," "within") precedes the name of an author or title to indicate a source. It is used like the French word *chez* to mean "in the works of" or "according to": *apud* Homer. It's appropriate for those occasions when you just want to impress classics teachers or elderly readers and it doesn't really matter whether anyone else understands.

....

Q. What is the correct way to write an endnote where the author has used a quote from a letter that appears in a volume of letters by someone else, and it appears as one of the book's appendixes? The book is *Delius: A Life in Letters, 1862–1908*. The editor is Lionel Carley. The letter quoted by the author of the essay I'm editing is from Jelka Delius, Frederick's wife. I've looked in chapter 14 of *CMOS*, but can't find anything that quite matches this. The author has put this:

> 1. "Jelka Delius: Memories of Frederick Delius," appendix 7 in Lionel Carley, ed., *Delius: A Life in Letters, 1862–1908*, vol. 1 (London: Scolar Press, 1983), 408–15.

Is this correct? Should it be

> 1. Jelka Delius, "Memories of Frederick Delius," in . . . ?

I hope I don't get scolded for submitting a silly query.

A. Your query is certainly not silly! A complex citation calls for thoughtful formatting. The author's version indicates that the book has an appendix titled "Jelka Delius: Memories of Frederick Delius." Your version would suggest something different: that the book has an appendix titled "Memories of Frederick Delius" that was written by Jelka Delius. Unless you have the book in front of you to confirm that you are right, you should leave this as the author wrote it.

There is danger in forcing citations into a set style regardless of their meaning. The goals are rather to convey the sources accurately and to tidy the punctuation and styling as much as you can without doing any damage. In Chicago style, your citation would look like this:

1. "Jelka Delius: Memories of Frederick Delius," appendix 7 in Frederick Delius, *Delius: A Life in Letters, 1862–1908*, ed. Lionel Carley (London: Scolar Press, 1983), 1:408–15.

Bibliographies

Q. What should I do if I'm missing certain bits of information for the bibliography? For example, I have many instances where I wrote down the date of a publication, but I can't find the volume and issue numbers. The same goes for the page numbers of the entire article; for example, I jotted down the number of the page I'm citing from but not the pages of the entire article. This is problematic, as I'm a historian completing my PhD dissertation on materials from the 1930s, and the sources I use are not available online.

A. I'd say you're in something of a pickle. First, try again online. Even if the text of an article isn't available, it's possible that you can find references to it that will include the missing information. Search for the article title and whatever information you have (journal title and year). Sometimes if you search for the journal, its year, and a page number (not the article title, which would limit the search), you will get hits that include the volume and issue numbers. Consider carefully whether to trust what you find. Try to confirm the information at more than one reputable site, keeping in mind that misinformation tends to replicate quickly online.

If you can't locate the information you need online, you'll have to dig it up the same way you did originally. Visit the libraries or archives where you did your research and find the sources. You might be able to ask a reference librarian by e-mail or phone to help you.

In some cases, it won't be disastrous to omit some information—for instance, if your note citation gives the year, volume, issue, and page number of the material you are quoting or referencing, the bibliography can do without the page range of the entire article. Unfortunately, even if a citation includes the year, page numbers alone aren't always helpful without an issue number. In that case, unless you are certain that the page numbers for that year number straight through without starting anew in each issue, you should consider dropping the source.

And need I scold you about not taking thorough notes on your sources?

....

Q. What if two authors with the same surname are cited, and their writings are published in the same year? How can I tell them apart when I am using the author-date citation system?

A. Use a first initial (R. Jones 2000; B. Jones 2000). If the initials are also the same, add a short title to your text citation (Jones, *Big Book*, 2000; Jones, "Little Article," 2000). If the works are by the same author, assign letters to the dates in your reference list and refer to them (Jones 2000a, 2000b).

....

Q. I have a question about the place of publication (country) to be included for a book in a reference list. *The Chicago Manual of Style* says to use the place that appears on the title page or copyright page of the book cited. My question is, if you need to specify the country but the name of the country has changed, do you use the name as it appears in the book, or do you use the current name? For example, if "Soviet Union" is shown on the title page, do you change it to "Russia" for the reference list entry?

A. Cite what is printed on the title page. Readers who are searching for a book need the details as they are printed and recorded in library records. Changing these details would be contrary to the purpose of a bibliography, which is to record sources and help readers locate them. (And aren't you glad you don't have to research political developments in every country in your reference list?)

....

Q. When using a pseudonym to hide the real name of an organization, how do you cite that organization's website in the references?

A. Hmm—fake URL? Encryption? Disappearing ink? (Is this a trick question?)

Q. I don't believe there is a standard Chicago/Turabian bibliographic citation format for video games yet. Is there?

A. *CMOS* and Turabian both contain examples of citations of video recordings that you can easily adapt to cite a video game. Please see *CMOS* 14.279 and Turabian, *A Manual for Writers of Research Papers, Theses, and Dissertations*, 17.8.5. Here's an example:

Cleese, John, Terry Gilliam, Eric Idle, Terry Jones, and Michael Palin. "Commentaries." Disc 2. *Monty Python and the Holy Grail*, special ed. DVD. Directed by Terry Gilliam and Terry Jones. Culver City, CA: Columbia TriStar Home Entertainment, 2001.

....

Q. At one time, the location of a publisher could be used to get a phone number via directory assistance. This is no longer how anyone would do it, and publishers have frequently moved, been acquired, and so forth, so the location is often highly ambiguous. Authors spend tens of thousands of hours annually looking up or making up publisher locations. I'm staring now at a copyeditor's request that I identify the location of Cambridge University Press—and the editor says it is because you insist on it. Can you give me any sane reason for this collective expenditure of effort and print? It would make me feel better, as it feels like an empty ritual of no contemporary value, engaged in by a field that is unaware of the digital era. Insistence on archaic rules brings to mind the replicant lament in *Blade Runner*, "Then we're stupid and we'll die."

A. We are so misunderstood! *CMOS* is not in the business of insisting on this or that. From our very first edition in

1906 we have stated very clearly that "rules and regulations such as these, in the nature of the case, cannot be endowed with the fixity of rock-ribbed law. They are meant for the average case, and must be applied with a certain degree of elasticity." As for place of publication, in scholarly research it can be useful in tracking the development of the literature within a discipline (especially in instances where publishers are old and obscure). In fact, it's not unusual for an academic to write a bibliography that includes only the place of publication for each work cited, without the publisher. When that happens, the editor or publisher must decide whether to require more information.

....

Q. I need help on how it would be easier to make a bibliography easier.

A. You could keep it short. You could find the references online and copy and paste them in so you don't have to type them. You could buy some software that helps format bibliographies. You could ask your mom to do it.

What if . . . ?

Q. We are currently revising the references of a book chapter and have come across the following problem: Two sources of the same year have the identical first seven authors, and we don't know how to differentiate them in the text (authors, year). In this case adding *a* and *b* to the year is not applicable, because starting with the eighth author, the authors are not the same. Should we list all eight names in both cases?

A. I'm afraid you're stuck with naming all the authors:

> (Grumpy, Doc, Happy, Sleepy, Bashful, Sneezy, Dopey, and Snow 2008)
>
> (Grumpy, Doc, Happy, Sleepy, Bashful, Sneezy, Dopey, and Queen 2008)

An alternative is to annotate the reference list with something like "In text, referred to as Grumpy et al. [1] 2008." Putting [1] after the author instead of *a* after the date indicates that Grumpy et al. [1] and Grumpy et al. [2] are different author groups, whereas 2008a and 2008b indicate different works of the same author group.

....

Q. I'm editing an entry in a list of references. We are asked to provide the date of access. The date the writer accessed the material was the very same day it was published; however, it was published in the Philippines, but it was accessed in the United States. So we have an access date that is one day before the date of publication. The publisher/client thinks this looks weird. Which option do you like best/dislike least:

(1) Keep the access date as is (one day before the publication date)

(2) Change the access date info to something like "Accessed on the date of publication"

(3) Change the access date to the date of publication

(4) Something else entirely

A. Your question is a new one for us! Answer 2 looks best, with the addition of the US date, in case it matters: accessed on the date of publication (May 6, 2012, in the US).

....

Q. I'm a production editor working on a novel and can't figure out the best way to present the epigraph source. The epigraph is "What I am is what I am," and the author wants the source to be "Lauryn Hill, 'A Rose Is Still a Rose.'" But in reality, the lyric is from the song "What I Am" by Edie Brickell & New Bohemians; Lauryn Hill sang that line in Aretha Franklin's recording of "A Rose Is Still a Rose." My first instinct is to just credit the epigraph as Edie Brickell & New Bohemians, but the book is urban fiction, and so referencing Lauryn Hill is important for the author. And I don't want to make it too complicated, since this is a novel and the epigraph should evoke a feeling in the reader, not make them ponder the finer points of music sampling. Any suggestions?

A. It would be sloppy and misleading to attribute the quote to Lauryn Hill. If Lauryn Hill sang the national anthem, would you attribute "O'er the land of the free and the home of the brave" to her? If the author is determined to quote Lauryn Hill, she should use a line from a Lauryn Hill song. Otherwise, she must credit whoever actually wrote that lyric, adding "as sung by Lauryn Hill" if she likes.

....

Q. I am copyediting a translation of a scholarly book. The translator and editor have decided to use two sets of notes: the author's notes, set as footnotes and numbered consecutively in Arabic numerals; and the translator's notes, set as endnotes and numbered consecutively in Roman numerals. Both the author's and translator's notes are quite lengthy, but especially the translator's notes. The translator and editor do not wish to use symbols for the author's notes, but having two sets of numbered references in the text seems awkward and somewhat confusing. Is there any other method one might use in such a case as this?

A. Although this isn't an impossible arrangement, the vision of roman numeral note callouts is a bit icky.[xxxviii] A better option might be to suppress numbers/symbols for the translator endnotes and instead key them to phrases in the text (*CMOS* 14.48). Or you could set all the notes (both author and translator) as endnotes (or footnotes) numbered in a single set, identifying notes written by the translator with a tag such as "—Trans."

Quotations and Dialogue

Q. Periods always go inside quotation marks. I have been told that the exception is when the matter within the quotation marks is a single number or letter. For example: The figure is impressed "1". Please tell me if I have been misinformed!

A. You are somewhat misinformed. The point is to move the period only when it's essential to make clear that the period is not included in the quoted matter, no matter how many letters or numbers are quoted:

Type in the code "W1.GH.748".
Please make the button read "Page Up".

Chicago style spells out the numbers one through one hundred, so a single digit is not likely to appear in quotation marks, but a single letter may be quoted with a period to no ill effect:

He demanded to know who ate the Twinkie, and she answered, "I."
Asked to give a middle initial, she replied, "X."

Q. I am editing a nonfiction manuscript of interviews with several fiction writers. The author uses ellipses (fairly often) to indicate a long pause in speech or thought. Is this a correct use of ellipses? How do you differentiate between long pauses and omissions of some lines within the transcribed conversation?
A. Yes, ellipses are properly used to indicate long pauses. If you also use them to indicate omissions, then you need to differentiate them and explain in a note how you do so. One way is to use a plain ellipsis for a pause . . . and a bracketed ellipsis [. . .] for an omission.

Q. Can I write dialogues without quotation marks as the author Frank McCourt did in his three memoirs?
A. Yes, you can.

Q. If court testimony is being quoted and the speaker does not often use correct grammar (repeats words, speaks in sentence fragments or sentences that don't logically follow, etc.), is it okay to change it extensively and use brackets to indicate the changes? Would a general disclaimer work?

A. It depends on your purpose. As a rule, court testimony must be rendered as spoken (as far as possible), because users require it to be accurate, not laundered through the preferences and judgments of an editor. In work that's not legal or scholarly you can take more liberties (with a disclaimer), although if your changes are extensive, paraphrases would probably be more elegant and readable.

Q. A manuscript I'm working on right now features a quote in running text which refers to the twentieth century. Since the quote is from the *New York Times*, it says "20th century"—which does not match the number style for the rest of our book. Is spelling out the number a permissible change to the quote?

A. No, this is not the sort of thing you should change in a quotation. But don't worry about appearing inconsistent; readers won't hold you responsible. They understand that you weren't available to copyedit everything that was ever written.

Q. I understand that commas should be used to introduce dialogue, typically in the fashion of "He said, 'Get my copy of *CMOS*!'" But what about instructions to begin a dialogue, make a statement, or ask a question? Should we use a comma, colon, or nothing in the following sentences:

Ask, "What's your name?"

Explain: "Today we are going to learn to say our names."
Say "I like apples."

The context is a teacher's manual instructing the reader on how to manage a lesson. My author has used a colon for many of these areas, but in similar sentences with longer introductory text she has instead used a comma or no punctuation as follows:

Explain to your students, "Today we are going to . . ."
Say in your best character voice "I'm ten!"

I find myself leaning toward the colon, but I'm conflicted; as this is a teacher's manual, there are many such sentences. After setting all instances on a page to colons, I then recoil in horror at the sight of so many colons on my screen! Is there a recommendation?

A. There is a lot of leeway for a writer in choosing punctuation before a quotation; it's nearly impossible to make a rule. In general, a colon is more emphatic; a comma or no punctuation is less disruptive. Usually an imperative works fine with no punctuation if the quoted material serves as a short and simple direct object:

Ask "What's your name?"
Say "I like apples."

Note that a comma may be used in those examples as well. If the quoted material after an imperative functions as an elaboration or demonstration of the command, rather than as a direct object, a colon is more apt:

Explain: "Today we are going to learn to say our names."

....

Q. A manuscript I am editing uses a lengthy extract from a source that uses brackets; in fact the original is sprinkled with unitalicized bracketed *sics*. What do I do? I don't want readers to think these interjections are added by us! I could say "brackets in original," but there are a couple of things we have had to add in brackets, too. Perhaps I should put a [*sic*] next to every [*sic*]. (Just kidding.)

A. Yes, adding a note "Brackets in original" is the right thing to do (although I love your idea of siccing the *sics*!). When you add your own comments within brackets, append "*Eds.*" (or just "*Ed.*") to the text to clarify.

....

Q. Microsoft Word just suggested I change "What do you mean 'unfortunately?'" to "What do you mean 'unfortunately'?" Should I tell Word to leave me alone, or am I mistaken in believing that, in American English, quotation marks envelop all neighboring punctuation?

A. Ah, you are mistaken. You must not include question marks and exclamation marks within the quotation marks unless they are part of the quotation. (Please see *CMOS* 6.70.) But since MS Word can't possibly divine the original quotation, yes, you may tell it to leave you alone.

CHAPTER SIX

"Holy metaphysics—we aren't that fancy"

....

....

Writers and students who are hit with the "Big Orange" for the first time might quail at the idea of applying its thousand-plus pages to their work. But whole chunks of *CMOS* have nothing to do with slippery issues of style or grammar or citing sources. Much of it covers the more creative decisions involved in putting together a book or article for publication, from how to list the authors to formatting, fonts, illustrations, and indexing. Not that these matters can't be just as controversial. Any increase in the number of choices available is bound to increase the number of opinions as well.

Authors, Titles, and Metadata

Q. Dear *CMOS* Staff, in a recent issue of one of our periodicals, I altered the original lineup of the names of five coauthors appearing under the title of an article and reordered them alphabetically. One of the coauthors is unhappy with this and requests, too late, to keep the original lineup, which, I assume, implicitly establishes some hierarchy in authorship. What should be my response to the unhappy coauthor?

A. Your response should be groveling apologies and a promise to issue a correction in the next issue of the journal and in the online version. Name order is important to authors in certain disciplines, as it indicates who is the lead author. It is meaningful to anyone who reads the paper or sees the citation on a résumé. Sometimes employment and promotion depend on having published a certain number of articles as the lead author. This is a truly regrettable error—the kind of error that can put the reputation of your periodical into question. Please make every effort to make amends.

....

Q. I thought at one point it was considered bad taste to include an author's degree on the front cover of a book (Steve Smith, PhD). But now I am wondering if that is the case. Any input? Is it just an individual decision?

A. It depends. It's unwarranted in scholarly writing, but if a book is for a mass audience and the degree gives potential readers an idea of the writer's qualifications, some publishers will want it stated: for instance, on a diet book written by a doctor, or a book on orchids written by a botanist. The author and editor should consult with the publisher's marketing department to decide what's best.

....

Q. I have written a book with twelve other authors. One of the authors is also the editor of the book. He has listed himself first as author/editor. I am thinking the authors should be listed first in alphabetical order and then the editor. Is this correct?

A. There's a fine old tradition for the authors to fight this out. Your suggestion would work, assuming that the entire book was authored by all twelve. If the book is a collection of chapters by individual authors, however, it's more conventional to list only the editor on the title page. The other authors appear in the table of contents and are perhaps listed on the book jacket flaps or back cover, depending on how famous they are.

....

Q. When a subsequent edition of a book is being published, is it proper to make any changes to the title of the book, or should the title appear exactly the same in all editions?

A. There's no law against changing the title of a book, but it can be awkward—think of the confusion. Everywhere the new title appears, it will have to be clarified: *Persuading with Power* (3rd edition of *A Woman's Guide to People-Pleasing*). Generally it's not a good idea unless for some reason the old title has become hopelessly out of date or offensive or problematic in some other way to the extent that confusion is preferable to retaining the old title.

....

Q. When the original author of a book has died and the original book is being revised by others, what is the best way to handle this on the title page? Should the original author be mentioned at all?

A. Horrors! When writers die, others don't get to grab their stuff and claim it belongs to them. The original writer is the *only* one whose name is required on the title page; the revisers' names come second ("Revised by") and are optional. If they want to be on a title page, tell them to write their own stuff.

Formatting

Q. In terms of full or ragged-edge justification of documents, which one is preferred for which type of document: business letter, research paper, sales and marketing materials?

A. Full justification is most often appropriate for typeset materials that have been professionally designed. All other materials should be ragged. In many cases you can judge for yourself: if full justification causes some lines to stretch out and others to squish together even when automatic hyphenation is turned on, it's better to go ragged.

Q. Does it matter what font style and size are used when submitting an essay for contest consideration?

A. Contest rules usually give guidelines for submitting work. Otherwise, it is standard in publishing to use 12-point type in a serifed font like Times New Roman. Use one-inch margins on all sides, no colors, no ALL CAPS anywhere. Indent the first line of each paragraph. Don't add space between paragraphs. Type a single space between sentences (not two). Editors want the text to be clear and to speak for itself. Prose decorated with bold and italics and caps looks unprofessional. If you are entering a contest, good luck!

....

Q. Does the font size of the footnotes need to be reduced in comparison to the main text font size?

A. In a manuscript, everything should be the same size. In a published document (whether typeset on paper or posted online), notes are usually set in smaller type.

....

Q. About two spaces after a period. As a US Marine, I know that what's right is right and you are wrong. I declare it once and for all aesthetically more appealing to have two spaces after a period. If you refuse to alter your bullheadedness, I will petition the commandant to allow me to take one Marine detail to conquer your organization and impose my rule. Thou shalt place two spaces after a period. Period. *Semper Fidelis.*

A. As a US Marine, you're probably an expert at something, but I'm afraid it's not this. *Status quo.*

....

Q. All right then! I'm steadfastly attempting to adopt the "one space after concluding punctuation" rule. It's not an easy task for a retired English teacher in his late sixties—one who preached the old rule to legions of eager-eyed scholars. Are there any retraining suggestions that assist the elder learner? I'm tired of correcting my continual errors. I am diligently trying, though.

A. Good for you! The easiest way might be for you to leave the mistakes in place until the document is finished, then use the Find and Replace feature to eliminate all double spaces. In the Find box, type two spaces, and in the Replace With box, type one space. Hit Replace All—and you're done. (And eventually, when your word processor regularly tells you that the search item was not found, celebrate!)

Illustrations

Q. Can you call out a figure from a subsequent section? For example, can you make a first reference to figures 3.9 through 3.12 in section 2.4? My stance is that you can't make a first-reference callout from the future, only from the current or a previous section. Calling out subsequent sections and appendixes (but not tables and figures) seems somehow different and not subject to this rule, which I might well have unknowingly made up.

A. This is one of many situations where it's not helpful to consider the general rule to be inflexible. If certain figures are mainly discussed in chapter 3 but the writer wants to point forward to them in chapter 2, it's perverse to either not allow it or force the writer to move the figures to chapter 2, away from the main discussion. Writers organizing a book should number the figures in the order they are discussed in the text, but after that, they should be able to refer to them anywhere the figures enhance the discussion.

....

Q. Is there a preferred way to refer in text to a specific column or row in a table? I tend to reuse the text in the column heading or stub entry rather than a number, just because I think it's clearer that way. For example, "See 'Countries' column" rather than "See column 4." Is that wrong?

A. Not at all. Some tables have numbered rows and columns, in which case "See column 4" is a perfect way to refer to the column. But a reference to a column number when the column heading is a word or phrase would not always be clear (e.g., which is column 1: the table stub or the first column after the stub?), and in a table with many columns, the reader would be forced to count the columns to find the data.

Q. I am using the double-numeration system recommended for heavily illustrated books (e.g., 4.1 for chapter 4, illustration 1). My problem is that there are two figures in the book's preface, which comes before an introduction without illustrations. Numbering such as P.1 or 0.1 could look awkward. How might I number those illustrations?

A. Both of your suggestions are commonly used. Neither is very pretty, but they are practical.

Q. This problem came up when copyediting a journal: on a page that is occupied by a broadside image and has a single footnote (to the caption of the image), should the footnote be oriented the same as the image and caption (i.e., 90 degrees from normal), or should it stay as regular?

A. It's not usual to footnote a caption rather than simply run the note into the caption with "Note:" in front of it, so you won't find a rule for this in *CMOS*. But to compound the oddity by having two strings of text at right angles to each other is probably not a good idea. It's almost always best, if possible, to set all the type on a page in such a way that it can be read continuously without turning the book.

Permissions, Credits, and Practical Issues

Q. In a self-published novel, do you need the permission of a certain company to mention a product name/brand or other trademarked title?

A. You don't need permission. Fortunately, we are all free to speak and write about Porsches and Jimmy Choos whether or not we can afford to buy them.

....

Q. A book endorsement was given by a bishop who has since been elevated to cardinal. The book will soon be reprinted (second edition). Should the endorsement printed on the back cover change to reflect his new title? Or should it remain as it was at the time the endorsement was given?

A. This is more of a marketing issue than editorial, and *CMOS* is silent on the subject. I believe marketing practice is to quietly update affiliations, since fancier titles are more impressive. If the statement is long out of date or very controversial, however, consider whether you might misrepresent the opinion of the blurber, in which case using the old affiliation (or a renewed statement from the blurber) would better represent the truth.

Q. I work at a major children's book publisher and have recently noticed a trend in creating books without any blanks at the end of the book. I would like to know if there is a rule on how many back-of-book blank pages are permissible in standard works of fiction (young-adult and middle-grade novels). At various adult publishers, I was taught that up to six pages is acceptable and that having at least a couple of blanks is actually preferable in order to allow for potential changes and additions during pass stages. But I can't seem to find anything online or in *CMOS* to support that. Thanks in advance for any light you can shed on this.

A. In conventional offset printing, large sheets of paper are folded into "signatures" of usually 16 or 32 pages (sometimes 8, or even 48) that are bound together and trimmed to make a book. For this reason, books have a page count that is a multiple of at least 8, and usually 16. Children's picture books have long been paged at 24, 32, 48, or 64 pages. Middle-grade books page out at larger multiples. Having blank pages in a book isn't a goal; it is simply unavoidable if the text and illustrations can't fill all the available space. And since it's expensive to tear out extra pages by hand, publishers turn a blind eye to the blanks. Digital printing doesn't involve these large sheets of paper, so if you are seeing a lot of self-published or print-on-demand books, they probably won't have any leftover pages.

....

Q. Hello. I've been charged with editing the credits in a new history textbook, but I'd like to know what you think should be done for crediting montage photographs. This is where two or more photographs have been morphed into one image for printing. Putting all the illustration credits on one line without some sort of distinguishing mark or word would make it difficult for interested persons to tell which part of the montage came from what company or photographer. What solution or alternative do you suggest?

A. Sometimes the pieces of a montage can be identified with terms like "clockwise from upper left" or "top, left to right; center, left to right; bottom, left to right." An alternative is to make a small line drawing of the components and number them so the credits can be keyed to the numbers. For elements superimposed or blended beyond distinction, there's not much point in trying to sort them out; just list the credits in alphabetical order. If it's essential to match each credit to its original, you might have to print thumbnail images of the original art as a guide.

....

Q. I work at a university press, and during a meeting of project editors we had a disagreement about the correct placement of the glossary. *CMOS* recommends that the glossary appear between the notes and bibliography. Although we'll accept this as your final answer, our question is why? Thank you!

A. Like many of the rules in *CMOS*, this one was begotten lo those many years ago. In an early edition of the *Manual*, the glossary was placed just so, and then that edition begat the next. The next edition begat the following one, and the following one begat the one after, and so on down unto these very days. Obviously, someone at the dawn of time thought it was a good idea, and no one in all the generations since has found reason to mess with it. And so that is why.

Indexing

Q. I know that endnotes are indexed. But which page number is listed—the page where the callout occurs, or the page where the actual endnote appears? If the latter, all subjects in endnotes on that page will have the same page number . . . the endnote page. Is that correct?

A. That's right. The idea of an index is to tell the reader where to locate the information. If you point her to the page of the callout, she will find nothing there but a callout, and she won't know the page number of the corresponding endnote, so she'll have to browse through the endnotes to find the right one. It's much more efficient (and kinder) to send her directly to the page where the note appears (along with the note number, of course).

....

Q. How should I index the name Teodoro Obiang Nguema Mbasogo?

A. In the absence of other information or advice (such as from the author), index unfamiliar unhyphenated names in the usual way, under the last name listed—in this case, Mbasogo. *CMOS* 16.71–87 covers rules for indexing special types of personal names.

....

Q. My indexing partner included names in the acknowledgments section in his index nominum. The text goes, "I am indebted to X and Z for materials or conversation that assisted my research for this article." Including X and Z in the index seems unnecessary to me. What do you think?

A. While it may not be necessary to include certain names in an index, it's common to allow a certain number of "vanity" entries, if there is room. This writer would like his colleagues or mentors to see their names when they look for them, and evidently he wasn't able to cite them in a more substantive way in the book.

....

Q. I'm creating a name index for a book on the history of Japanese imperial rule, which is heavy on references to Japanese deities. The deities are discussed numerous times in connection with the early Japanese emperors, for example as part of the first emperor's lineage. I believe only people should be in the name index, but are there any exceptions, such as this one?

A. If you are the author of the book, you get to decide what to put in your index. If you're writing the index for someone else, that person is the best one to decide. If deities are to be included, you might rename the index "Index of Persons and Deities." Or you could have a separate glossary of deities. Don't worry about conventions and exceptions. Think about what the readers of this book will need, and then create it for them.

....

Q. Hello! When indexing a book that names the same person literally hundreds of times (it's about this person's philosophy), is *passim* correct in the index? Same Q about his works; some of the famous works are named or referenced dozens, if not hundreds of times.

A. Imagine yourself using this index to find something. What good is *passim*? A reader already knows that X is mentioned throughout the book. Professional indexers disagree whether it even makes sense to have an entry for the main subject of a book, but if you do, it must be broken up into many subentries and possibly sub-subentries, so readers can find what they're after. (In fact, any index entry that consists of more than five or six page numbers should be further broken down into subentries.) Some indexers of biographies create an entry for the person's name, but within it they list only passages that relate to the person's life events (birth, marriage, death), which could not easily be listed elsewhere in the index. Some indexers also put under the person's name "Works. *See titles of individual works*." Your questions show that you would profit from learning more about indexing before you go further. I suggest you read the indexing chapter of *CMOS*.

Using a Style Manual

Q. Somewhere I picked up the "fact" that the numbering system used in the *Chicago Manual of Style* was modeled after that of *Tractatus Logico-Philosophicus*. Is this "fact" a fact or have I slipped a cog? Is it mentioned in the *CMOS*?

A. Holy metaphysics—we aren't that fancy. *CMOS* simply numbers each paragraph, starting over in each chapter; section 7.85 is the eighty-fifth paragraph of chapter 7. Wittgenstein's system provides a complex nesting of his statements about his seven propositions. In the *Tractatus*, proposition 6 is elaborated in section 6.1, which is further elaborated in 6.11, and even further in 6.111. Thus you can read across levels for surface understanding, or down into them for greater detail.

....

Q. I am the first and only technical writer at this company. Since they do not have any style guides, I know legally there are no issues in using the *Chicago Manual of Style*. But is it legally OK to use the *Microsoft Manual of Style*?

A. I suppose that depends what you use it for. (How heavy is it?)

....

Q. Will there ever be a word processing program designed to use only *The Chicago Manual of Style*?

A. If you could put all the monkeys in the world on all the computers in the world, with all the tech consultants in the world, maybe, at some point in infinity, there would be such a program.

CHAPTER SEVEN

"Aaagh!" to "argh!" to "aahhh!"

....

ALPHABETIZING ✳ IN THE WEEDS OF EDITING ✳
SPECIAL CHARACTERS ✳ URLS ✳ YOU COULD LOOK IT UP ✳
THINGS THAT FREAK US OUT

....

A style manual—even one as big as *CMOS*—can't cover everything. If you encounter an oddball issue such as the ones we receive via the Q&A, try not to panic. Our hope is that you'll navigate your way to the most relevant section of the *Manual* and extrapolate from what you read there. Look it up in the index, the tables of contents, or the online search box, and once you've read our advice and devised your own solution, make a note of it so you can do the same thing if the issue arises again in that document.

Alphabetizing

Q. In letter-by-letter alphabetization, is it correct to assume that articles, prepositions, and conjunctions are not alphabetized? E.g., would Albert the Great precede Albert of Saxony?

A. Every letter is taken into account in letter-by-letter alphabetizing. Please see the examples at *CMOS* 16.61. E.g.,

newsletter
News of the World (Queen)
news release

....

Q. As the editor of my workplace magazine, I have to alphabetize lists of donors and members. I can find no references to the following situation in the *Manual*: a man and woman donate as a couple (and thus will be included as one entry on the list) but have different last names. This seems to be an etiquette question, but exploring those references has not helped either. Should the names be alphabetized by whichever partner's name is listed first on the form submitted by the donors or by the man's last name? Please share your insight.

A. By the *man's* last name? That would be one way to do it. (How eager are you for the women who wrote the checks to donate again?) But it would be more politic to follow the order listed on the form.

....

Q. I have a disagreement with a coworker about how to alphabetize street names with foreign words in them. I live in San Diego, so there are a lot of Spanish street names. I, for example, would file Via Hacienda under *V*. She argues that because *Via* means "Street," it should be under *H* instead. She reasons that if it were House Street, we would file it under *H*. My argument is that since we are not speaking Spanish, we should follow standard English alphabetizing rules.

A. You are right; there could be any number of foreign-language terms among the street names in San Diego, and unless all readers knew all the languages, the list would be useless. You can see that the city government of San Francisco puts Via Bufano under V in its street guide (https://data.sfgov.org/, under Geographic Locations and Boundaries: Street Names). Another solution is to list such names in both locations, or to put in blind entries:

Via Hacienda. *See* Hacienda, Via
or
Hacienda, Via. *See* Via Hacienda

....

Q. I have an author with (let's say) the last name St. James and am having a hard time figuring out the correct form for her bibliography entry. Is it correct to alphabetize under St. James, Bertha? Or James, St. Bertha? HELP!!

A. Having the surname St. James doesn't make one Saint James—or Saint Bertha; Bertha's surname starts with *S*.

In the Weeds of Editing

Q. Dear *CMOS*: In a business directory, each company's page has a section for office locations. It just lists the place-names, not addresses. For example, the places where one company has offices are

—Illinois
—Madison Avenue
—Nevada
—San Diego

—Silicon Valley

—Wall Street

My concern as a copyeditor is that the locations are a mix of states, cities, and business districts. Is it being persnickety to edit to

—Illinois

—Madison Avenue, New York City, New York

—Nevada

—San Diego, California

—Silicon Valley, California

—Wall Street, New York City, New York

My problem with the second list is that non-Americans wouldn't know, and maybe wouldn't care, what "level" of geography Illinois and Nevada are (the directory is to be marketed outside the country). I could list the states first and put the specific area in parentheses: California (Silicon Valley), but for an IT company, the important detail is Silicon Valley and not California. Thanks for your advice!

A. I agree with you that the list makes a copyeditor blink, but unless the main client base for this company is copyeditors, it's probably best not to insult anyone's intelligence with too much information. You might add "NYC" to the street names, if you think anyone will be puzzled.

....

Q. I enjoy reading the monthly Q&A. The answers often seem to tell the questioners to use some common sense, that there isn't one right answer necessarily for every situation, and that comprehensibility trumps consistency and being a stickler. Certainly, though, there are times when there is a right answer. Do you have a philosophy or recommendations for how to distinguish those situations from the rest?

A. We're working on an app for that; meanwhile, you'll have to trust your judgment.

Q. In the references section of a paper I'm editing, I found a misspelled word. I checked the original journal and found that it was published with this mistake. Should I correct the typo or leave it as is? My colleague says the typo should stay because this is how it appeared in print originally. Thanks a lot!

A. You may correct the typo. (Of course, you must be very, very certain that it's actually a typo before you change it.) If an error has important implications that you want to point out, you can reproduce the error and write [*sic*] after it, but it's not nice to do this just to point out that someone made a mistake.

Q. We are editing a scientific book. We have to follow UK spelling. Per the dictionary, *sulfur* is the US spelling and *sulphur* is the UK spelling. But in one chapter the author has used *sulfur* and in another chapter *sulphur*. Since we are following UK spelling, can we change *sulfur* to *sulphur*? Or, per *CMOS*, since the IUPAC-recommended spelling is *sulfur* irrespective of UK or US spelling, can we change *sulphur* to *sulfur*?

A. Good grief. You can't lose—just pick one.

Q. I'm currently editing a manuscript for a children's fiction book that has been written in present tense. A few months back, when Americanizing another manuscript, I changed it from present tense to past tense. Although I have no citable rule to back up my decision, I feel as if these books should be written in past tense. Present tense just sounds odd for children's fiction. Is this a paradigm that I should be willing to ignore, or is there an arguable reason that I have this tendency? I would appreciate any rationale you have to offer.

A. The choice of tense is so personal, and so critical to a fiction writer's purpose, that it would be rash to restrict an entire genre like children's books to a single tense. Many excellent children's books have been written in the present tense. If you feel that the past tense would improve the book, however, rewrite a paragraph or two and send it to the author for discussion.

....

Q. How do you spell out the sound of a scream? I've seen everything from "aaagh!" to "argh!" to "aahhh!" Please tell me there's a limit to the number of times one can repeat letters!

A. There is a limit to the number of times one can repeat letters! Unfortunately, the limit is different in almost every case.

....

Q. My copyeditor has changed "as described below" to "as described following" and has changed "as noted above" to "as noted before." Is my usage correct, or at least acceptable? I have never seen the usage the copyeditor has suggested. Is this usage becoming a trend, and what does *CMOS* think about it? Thank you.

A. Your usage is correct and acceptable; your editor's changes are awkward and unidiomatic. Some overeager editors remove directions like *above* and *below* in the fear that once the text in question is typeset it might end up directly across on a facing page or at the top of a page overleaf, in which case the terms *above* and *below* will not be literally true. If your pointers refer to illustrations (whose positioning is beyond your control), such precautions are reasonable. Otherwise, it's silly to think that readers don't understand that *above* means "before" and *below* means "after." One way to negotiate this might be to consider whether phrases like "as described below" or "as noted above" are truly needed. They suggest a writer who doesn't trust his readers to keep reading or remember what they've read.

....

Q. I see the word *that* in constructions where clarity would not be diminished without it. An example in the Q&A was "He thinks that, if he asks for directions, his membership in the brotherhood of men will be revoked." I consider "He thinks if he . . ." correct.

A. Both constructions are correct, but leaving out *that* can lead to confusion whenever the next noun can be mistaken for an object of the verb (I judged for thirty years the county fair pickling contest was rigged). It's safer to include *that*. You can always reconsider if it is awkward for any reason.

Special Characters

Q. Is there a standard for replacing an expletive with special $%!# characters?

A. Although there isn't a steady demand for masked expletives in scholarly prose, this is weirdly one of our frequently asked questions. (I have to wonder who is reading the Q&A—and what they are writing.) The symbols are fine for cartoons and e-mail messages, where you may arrange them in whatever order pleases you. In formal prose, however, we find that a 2-em dash makes a d——d fine replacement device.

....

Q. I wonder what your ruling is on using Latin-based (but non-Latin) characters as part of a person's name. At my job, I am often required to write about Turkish Prime Minister Erdoğan. English publications usually write it as Erdogan, but this has the side effect of people pronouncing it "Er-do-gan" and looking foolish. I would argue we should write it Erdoğan, as this more closely reflects the name's pronunciation (as well as its actual spelling), and the alphabet is still comprehensible to an English speaker. However, what is your take?

A. If your typesetters can set the correct letter, by all means use it. Although writers who quote you may type a plain *g*, not knowing how to reproduce the special character, there's nothing you can do about that. Whenever it's appropriate, help your readers out by providing the pronunciation in parentheses or in a note.

Q. I notice confusion in publications in regard to whether a space should precede and/or follow relation signs. My suspicion is that it is <10 km but $p < .001$.

A. That's right: there is no space after a relation sign when it acts as a modifier (e.g., Results hold for all quantities <10 km), but there is space on both sides when it acts as a verb (e.g., Results hold for all quantities such that $p < .001$).

URLs

Q. In running text, is it necessary to include a website's domain extension? "The video on YouTube.com showed a cat," for example, looks incredibly stilted. The publication I'm working on is scholarly—but not intended specifically for grandmothers. Can I get rid of the ".com" if it's clear that a website is being referred to?

A. Hey, there are grandmas who could tell you that you should be careful about shortening your references, because not all sites end in .com. If the exact site (like YouTube) can be located reliably in an online search, fine, but if you're referring to a more commonly used name like Best Foods, there could be any number of websites with the same name that end in .net, .org, .biz, or other extension.

....

Q. In a story where the last text provides a URL, website, or e-mail address, should it not have a period at the end? I find sometimes clicking on the URL does not take one directly to the displayed location if a period follows.

A. Yes, you must put a period at the end of a sentence, even if the sentence ends with a URL (or e-mail address). If it's essential that the link be clickable, make sure that the code that determines the hyperlink destination does not include the final period. (Most word-processing programs allow you to edit hyperlinks, even if they've been created automatically.) If you don't have that option, then consider moving the URL so that it doesn't fall at the end of a sentence or anywhere else that punctuation might be required.

....

Q. An online course I am building has many references to external websites. How should these be presented? I have been told to use both the name of the website and the URL but neither one should be hyperlinked. This sounds a little weird to me. Is there an official "right" way to do this?

A. There is no official right way to do this. Sometimes URLs are spelled out online because the material is meant to be printed out—perhaps by teachers, to hand out in class—and the readers won't necessarily have access to the Internet while they're reading. Sometimes URLs are spelled out because they serve as examples (such as at our website) and aren't meant to be accessed. Try to find out the purpose of the material you're working with. If it's purely online content, then you might point out that using URLs instead of links is going to look amateurish.

....

Q. Have you established any rules for breaking web addresses at ends of lines? I would be inclined to break at the slash where possible, with no hyphen (keeping the address intact), but what about the "dots"? Example: eic.edu.gov.on.ca/html /dsbmaps.html (I've got another one that's a line and a quarter long!).

A. In printed publications, we recommend breaking before a period and most other marks of punctuation—including a slash (but not a double slash; always break after "http://"). This helps make it clear that the URL has not come to an end. Never add a hyphen to break a URL. For more detailed information, including examples, see paragraph 14.12 in *CMOS* 16.

You Could Look It Up

Q. Please help me! I am arguing with my publisher. I say that *back seat* is correct, and she says it's *backseat*. Please tell me which is correct, and thank you.

A. A publisher and a writer who between them can't find a dictionary? *Merriam-Webster's Collegiate Dictionary* (11th ed.) says *backseat*.

....

Q. I don't see anything in your online guide about how to cite art exhibition catalogs. I frequently need to cite them. Did I miss it in the guide? If not, would you consider adding it to your guide? It would be helpful. Thanks.

A. Exhibition catalogs are cited like books. Please see *CMOS* 14.250. You can find this in the index under both *exhibi-*

tions and *catalogs* or by typing either of those words into the Search box. (We're teaching how to fish today.)

....

Q. In the latest Q&A on your website, I noted that an answer contained the word *lowercased*. Is this really a verb or another example of a noun erroneously transformed into a verb? I cannot imagine that you would make such an error, but I have never heard that verb before!

A. *Lowercase* is a fine verb; you can look it up in a dictionary. And in any case, I don't know any rule against making a noun into a verb. Writers and speakers of good English have been verbifying for a long time, and sometimes it works out well. I understand your resistance, though. I winced recently when I heard someone say, "Let's see if we can solution that."

....

Q. I wonder which you think is best: Key Lime pie, Key lime pie, or key lime pie?

A. I'm actually partial to pecan, but if you're asking about spelling, consult a dictionary: *Merriam-Webster's Collegiate* (11th ed.) prefers lowercasing, noting that *Key* is often capped.

....

Q. In two different writers' group meetings, two writers told me that *OK* should be spelled *okay*. Both said it was because that's what *Chicago Manual of Style* calls for, but I can't find this in *CMOS*. My training (newspaper, mind you, so AP style) is to use first-listed spelling, and *OK* is first-listed in every dictionary I checked. Has Chicago ever specified *okay*, or are these ladies confusing their publishers' house styles with that of *CMOS*?

A. *CMOS* doesn't specify, but as it happens, the manual uses *OK* twice (at 2.66 and 7.48; 2.113 doesn't count) and does not use *okay* at all. The Q&A uses both spellings. (You can learn all this by typing the words into the Search box at *CMOS Online*.) We follow *Merriam-Webster's Collegiate* (11th ed.), which puts *OK* as the first spelling—but that does not mean it is preferred. Rather, *okay* is an equal variant (also standard). Your writer friends are misguided, in any case. It's rarely wrong to use an accepted spelling. Consistency within a document can be assured by using a style sheet.

....

Q. On so many levels it seems true journalism is dead, but what required reporters to take out the English language with them? I refer to the constant phrasing similar to the following: "The defendant PLEADED not guilty at the arraignment." Have these people never seen or heard the word "pled," or did I miss a memo?

A. Sorry—you missed the memo. (You can also check usages like this in a good dictionary.)

....

Q. Why is it so hard to find things in *CMOS*?

A. It must be just one of those things. If only there were a search box, or an index . . .

Things That Freak Us Out

Q. I am overwhelmed by the task of alphabetizing a list of book titles, as many of the titles have colons, commas, and in some cases, dashes separating the title and subtitle. It is all getting to be a bit much for me. Given the large number of titles I am working with, I would prefer to ignore all punctuation, but what to do in the following situation? Would I ignore the dash, the comma, and the colon and move on to the word following *Band* in the title? Believe it or not, these are actual examples: *The Beatles—Rock Band*; *The Beatles, Rock Band*; *The Beatles: Rock Band*; *The Beatles Rock Band*.

A. Normally the only punctuation marks that matter in alphabetizing are parentheses and commas, but in the case of titles with subtitles, it might make sense to promote the colon to primary importance. In that case, *The Beatles: Rock Band* would come first. After that, decide the order you like for other punctuation marks and note it in your style sheet. In titles, the dash and comma sometimes serve the same role as a colon (separating the title and subtitle), so you might put them next. Please note, too, that this issue does not fall into the category of stuff that is important to readers. However you order these nearly identical titles, they are all in one convenient location for the reader. It's not worth your sanity to let it overwhelm you.

....

Q. A styling trend lately that is keeping me up at night is a failure to identify new paragraphs by either a line break or an indent.

This new line of text, for example, is the sort of thing I mean. Is this a new paragraph or not? How can one tell? Does it matter?

I first spotted this ambiguous formatting in ad copy (which at the time I presumed to be bulleted points without the bullets), and then in corporate communications. But tragically, yesterday I read a review on the back of a novel that did the same thing: a new line for every sentence without letting me know if it was a new paragraph or not.

I'm already annoyed by the look of this e-mail! Please help!

A. I suspect that this style began to appear unintentionally as a result of inept word processing and has by now become a fad. A styled paragraph indent (instead of a typed tab) can get lost when the electronic file is converted to another application on its way to typesetting. In some display contexts (like book jackets) it might succeed as a hip design tactic, but in text it's difficult to read. Although I'm not sure the trend qualifies as "tragic," it's certainly unhelpful to those of us who need our sleep.

....

Q. Oh, English-language gurus, is it ever proper to put a question mark and an exclamation mark at the end of a sentence in formal writing? This author is giving me a fit with some of her overkill emphases, and now there is this sentence that has both marks at the end. My everlasting gratitude for letting me know what I should tell this person.

A. In formal writing, we allow both marks only in the event that the author was being physically assaulted while writing. Otherwise, no.

Q. My joining your site was prompted by entry 8.40, "Centuries and Decades," of your 14th edition. Your sample decades were 1800–1809 and 1910–19, and those examples make no sense to me. Decades must have ten years; decades can't skip years; decades can span neither millennia nor centuries as you have them doing in your examples; e.g., 1800 is the last year of the 18th century, not the first year of the 19th century, and the second decade of the 20th century is 1911–20, not 1910–19. I don't want to get off on the wrong foot, but isn't precision an essential ingredient in all writing before style considerations? Also, should writing style be based on popular culture rather than logic? I'm troubled by this entry in your manual and I'd appreciate your letting me know how you justify it.

A. Welcome to *CMOS* 16 (and the twenty-first century)! As any linguist will confirm, in both grammar and style matters, convention often outweighs logic, and there is little to be done about it. If you decide to start a campaign to impose logic on the designation of decades and millennia, we wish you well. In the meantime, you'll be happy to know that both the 15th and 16th editions of *CMOS* acknowledge your system: "Note also that some consider the first decade of, for example, the twenty-first century to consist of the years 2001–10; the second, 2011–20; and so on. Chicago defers to the preference of its authors in this matter" (9.37 and 9.34, respectively).

....

Q. I am writing a novel. How do I write a title of a song in the body of the work (caps, bold, underline, italics, etc.)? Example: The Zombies' "She's Not There" looped in his head.

A. Noooo! Now that song is looping in my head ("but it's too late to say you're sorry . . ."). Use quotation marks. Thanks a lot.

....

Q. Contracts often employ defined terms in quotes and parentheses, e.g., ABC Corp. (the "Seller") shall sell ten widgets to XYZ Corp. (the "Buyer"). When drafting such a contract, I always put a period after the close parenthesis if it is the end of the sentence, such as in the above example. But it's like listening to nails on a chalkboard to me to have a period essentially (ignoring the parenthetical) follow the period employed in an abbreviation. What do you recommend?

A. Yoga?

....

Q. How do you recover from a real proofreading blooper—the kind that has everyone in gales and is terribly embarrassing?

A. Naturally, we have very little experience with this. Is there absolutely no way to blame it on someone else? If not, you probably should keep a low profile until it blows over. Lucky for you, proofreaders automatically have a fairly low profile.

....

Q. My library shelves are full. I need to make some difficult decisions to make space for new arrivals. Is there any reason to keep my *CMOS* 14th and 15th editions?

A. What a question. If you had more children, would you give away your firstborn? Find a board and build another shelf.

Index

quotations, 63–64

See also author-date citation
  style; bibliographies; notes
  (endnotes and footnotes)

city of, 21

clarity, 45, 98

clichés, 56

co-, 20

coauthors, order of, 78–79

college, 22

colons

  with independent clauses, 41

  in place of a semicolon, 40

  before a quotation, 75–76

commas

  before *and*, 31

  with appositives, 48

  with compound objects, 31–32

  before dialogue, 75

  in e-mail greetings, 30–31

  before *if*, 31

  before *including*, 46–47

  between independent clauses, 31

  after introductory phrases, 32

  with nonrestrictive phrases,
    47–49

  optional, 30–31, 32, 47–48

  parenthetical, 52

  placement, 31

  before quotations, 76

  serial, confused with commas in
    nonrestrictive phrases, 49

common sense, in applying guidelines. *See* editorial judgment

compound objects and subjects

  me or *I*, 55

  position of *me*, 55

  possessive form, 14

compound phrases

  hyphenating, 6–8

  noun plus participle, 35

  number plus noun, 34

  permanent, 5, 6

comprehensibility, over consistency,
  96

consistency, 2, 96, 104. *See also*
  inconsistency

context, role in understanding, 57

contractions, 41

contracts, defined terms in, 108

convention versus logic, 107

copyeditor versus *copy editor*, 6

correctness

  in bad writing, 32

  versus common sense, 32–33

  of idioms, 52

  versus ickiness, 12, 56, 73

  multiple versions of, 1, 33

country names, former, citing, 68

couples' names, alphabetizing in
  lists, 93

courting versus dating, 57–58

court testimony, quoting, 74–75

dangling modifiers, 32, 55–56

Dao De Jing, 49

date of access, in advance of date of
  publication, 71–72

decades, 107

degrees. *See* academic degrees

DeLillo, Don, 44

department names, 25–26

diacritics, 99

dialogue, without punctuation, 74

dictionaries

  for checking usage, 104

  disagreement among, 6, 19

  for styling compound words, 6

  use of, 26, 43, 52–53, 102–4

digital printing, and page counts, 86

display type, 106

dissertations, applying the rules to,
  3, 39, 59–60, 66

documentation. *See* citations

dollar sign, with numbers, 10

double genitive (double possessive), 15

double-numeration system, for
  illustrations, 84

double prepositions, 52

french dressing, 26

gender-biased (gender-inclusive)
language, 49–50, 51, 93
generic terms, casing of, 20, 24–25
geographical adjectives, nonliteral,
26
German shepherd, 26
glossary, placement of, 87
governmental bodies, capitalization, 20–21
grammar-checking software, 77
grammar superstitions, 51
grammar versus style, 1, 43
graphic interchange format (GIF), 5
Greek, 17–18

had had, 56
happy medium, 46
Harry Potter, 27–28
headline style, 12, 25, 28
Hebrew, 17–18
her, herself. See pronouns
Hill, Lauryn, covering Edie Brickell
& New Bohemians, 72
him, himself. See pronouns
honorifics, 21–22. See also titles, of
offices
hours, inclusive, 10
house styles, 104
hyperlinks, editing, 101. See also
URLs
hyphenation
automatic, and justification, 81
and capitalization, 20
as a last resort, 33–34
of number + noun modifiers,
34–35, 35–36
of phrasal adjectives, 35
of prefixes, 20
of proper names, 35, 36

ibid., 63
ickiness, 12, 73. See also correctness
idiom, 15, 52

i.e., in running text, 40
illustrations. See figures
imperative, with quotations, punctuation for, 76
inanimate objects, with possessive,
15–16
including, comma before, 46–47
inclusive numbers, 10, 38–39
inconsistency
institutional, 13
needless worry over, 26, 36
in numbers, 8–9, 75
See also consistency
indents, for paragraphs, styled
versus tabbed, 106
indexing
acknowledgments, 88–89
biographies, 89–90
endnotes, 88
proper names, 88–89
purpose, 88
initialisms. See abbreviations, acronyms, initialisms
Internet, searching, 66–67
interviews, ellipses for pauses in, 74
introductory phrases, commas
after, 32
it, referring to the subject, 54
italics
in company names, 17
in non-Latin scripts, 17–18
versus quotation marks, for
words used as words, 17
its versus it's, 54–55

Jackson, Shelley, "Skin" (short
story), 62
jargon, 43
judgment. See editorial judgment
justification, full versus ragged, 81
justifying editorial decisions, 44

Key lime pie, 103

language regulators, 45–46